'TALKING ANIMALS'

(Dictio Grex)

A Primer on the History of Slavery

2010

Harve E. Rawson

authorHOUSE®

AuthorHouse™
1663 Liberty Drive
Bloomington, IN 47403
www.authorhouse.com
Phone: 1-800-839-8640

First published by AuthorHouse   3/26/2010

ISBN: 978-1-4520-0036-7 (e)
ISBN: 978-1-4520-0035-0 (sc)

Printed in the United States of America
Bloomington, Indiana

This book is printed on acid-free paper.

Special Thanks

to

Cathy Dornblaser

Who talked me into writing this book

and then graciously critiqued,

edited and proofread

the manuscript

and thanks also to Patricia Crippins and Kathy Chahrouri
who kindly offered many helpful suggestions

FOREWORD

I have had an interest in slavery ever since I was an adolescent in southern Missouri. I remember a fellow employee on my first full-time job telling me his great grandfather had owned a slave back in Neosho, Missouri, and how that slave got loaned out to neighbors when they needed an extra hand. It was hard for me to conceive that the very ground I was standing on was once populated with human merchandise that could be sold as casually as we now buy an automobile or a refrigerator.

I had grown up in a race-segregated society and wondered what the origins were of Negroes (as they were then called) having to sit in the balcony at the movie theater (even though they paid the same admission), not being allowed to eat in 'white-only' restaurants, having to sit in separate sections on the busses and trains, and only being allowed to use 'colored' restrooms and water fountains. It all seemed kind of silly even then, but I never questioned it.

Later, when in Antioch College, our 'gang' of good friends who went drinking together included a young black man from New Jersey. One night, with too much beer in me, I resorted to my Missouri origins and was telling a story about life in Webb City. Suddenly, I realized I had used the 'n' word in telling the tale and quickly looked at my black friend who was as embarrassed as I was. When I hurriedly apologized, he graciously sloughed it off, but somehow our relationship was never quite the same and I deeply regretted it. The incident made me aware I was a racist without realizing it up until that time. It was also then I became conscious of the terrible price Americans pay for their history of racial slavery, i.e., racism.

Years later, I began to travel all over the world. Among other things, I visited the many edifices, roads, aqueducts and amphitheaters thousands and thousands of slaves had built during the long-running Roman Empire; the 'door of no return' at Goree Island off the coast of Senegal where slaves were sold by the pound and then shipped away to the Americas under such indescribable conditions that a third perished on the journey; and the suffocating 'holding pens' of the famous slave market at Zanzibar where thousands of Africans changed hands every week of the year. I also visited the island in Viet Nam where coolies were sold like cattle for the French plantations south of there; the 'slave suqs' of Morocco where every Thursday slaves were commonly auctioned off up until the beginning of the 20th century; and the 'freedom post' in Bahrain where the British had emancipated slaves clear up until 1971 in the old Gulf Trucial States. Other journeys let me visit the sun-soaked farms of India where 'debt slaves' work the land, their labor mortgaged generation after generation to the land owners there (who to this day refuse to label this 'slavery') and the old gold mines of Peru where first Indian slaves and later black slaves lived at best a decade after being sold to the mine owners and chained in place within the deep holes in the ground often to never see daylight again. All over the world slavery had left its mark.

But any American doesn't have to travel far to be aware of slavery. My home was right on the Ohio River where Kentucky joins Indiana - 'Signal Rock' told the Kentucky slaves when to cross if they dared and seek freedom in the north. To do so, some of them traveled at night right up a creek bed (that ran through my property) so the dogs of the bounty hunters wouldn't get them.

As a psychologist studying the phenomenon of slavery, I became fascinated with the incredible human spirit, the indomitable determination, the amazing adaptation and, most of all, the enduring optimism slaves exhibited over the ages amidst their terrible suffering including much physical agony and unbelievable psychological angst. Most slaves lost everything: their identities, their friends, their families, and their sense of self-worth. They often ended up in places totally alien to them where they understood neither the language nor the customs.

Invariably they were thrust into the bottom of the heap both socially and economically. Most had no hope of eventual freedom, some had been born into it, and those having children witnessed their offspring sold off just like they had been.

Surely many slaves must have suffered what psychologists and psychiatrists now diagnose as posttraumatic stress disorder (PTSD) and indeed slaves often seemed to exhibit many of the same symptoms we see today in those suffering severe trauma. Some tried to kill themselves when they realized what had happened to them; some killed themselves before they could even be turned into slaves. Some limped out their lives suffering from chronic depression; some slowly died of lack of interest in living; some couldn't comprehend the treatment they received or what was expected of them; some were overwhelmed that fellow humans who now owned them perceived them as subhuman no better than beasts of burden and devoid of human emotions or aspirations. Perhaps the best adjusted were slaves who had been born into it - they benefitted from never knowing any other condition outside of being owned. But most slaves did survive; most did what they could to achieve what happiness was possible in their servile state; and some even managed to escape it altogether either through manumission, a successful escape, or even a merciful death.

Slavery is a sad tale of man's inhumanity to man. But this book is dedicated to all those millions of slaves who survived and passed their great genes on to us.

Harve E. Rawson
2010

CONTENTS

INTRODUCTION

If you want to know what a slave looks like, look in the mirror! Yes, that's right. Historically, it is highly likely that at least one of your ancestors, somewhere, sometime, was a slave.

If you have some German, Spanish, Celtic, Italian, African, Slavic or Semitic blood in you, you might have an ancestor living at the time of the Roman Empire - it is estimated that at one time one in three or four people living in the Roman Empire at any given time were slaves.

If you have some Oriental blood in you your ancestors might have lived in Korea, where at one time up to a third of all peoples there were slaves; or in China or Siam where in some areas there were more slaves than free men.

If you have some Scandinavian blood in you some ancestor or another might have been a thrall - the most common classification for people in lifetime bondage who numbered in the hundreds of thousands.

If your ancestors hailed from almost anywhere in Africa (North, South, East, West) you would be a rarity indeed if some ancestor somewhere down the line wasn't a slave.

With very few exceptions the history of mankind runs parallel with the history of slavery. Humankind's penchant to own and control other humans for their own gain seems to be as old as the dawn of time. Indeed, historical anthropologists yearly unearth more and more ancient societies that practiced slavery and archeologists seem amazed where they cannot find any overt evidence of slavery in their excavations, so much so they feel they have missed something in their studies. Some writings from ancient sources (e.g., the Jewish sect of the Essenes) claim owning another human being is a bad thing and should be eliminated, but it's hard to find evidence they actually practiced what they preached since slavery was a common institution all around them. In fact, the suggestion that slavery is a moral issue is fairly recent, probably less than two or three centuries old, as compared with the thousands of years before that. Prior to this, slavery is seen as the natural order of human society (clearly stated by both Plato and Aristotle) and any debate over slavery was largely limited to proper discipline and treatment of slaves. The moral question as to whether humans should literally own other humans was rarely if ever raised.

Nowhere is this more clearly demonstrated than in the major religious writings over the centuries. Jewish holy writings talk about proper treatment of slaves and possible manumission of slaves under certain conditions but never tackle whether slavery itself is good or bad. Christian writings about slavery (mainly authored by Paul of Tarsus) limit themselves to encouraging slaves to accept their lot in life, obey whoever owns them, and to look forward to a better life following death (although even there is it not made clear whether they would remain slaves or not in their heavenly afterlife). Nowhere in the Old or New Testament is there even a hint that slavery itself is wrong or immoral or un-Christian. The Islamic Koran, proclaimed somewhat later, is more specific about slavery: followers of the Prophet should treat their human property with respect and consideration; manumission of a longtime and faithful slave brings honor to the master; "believers" should not be enslaved under normal circumstances. But nowhere in the Koran is there even a suggestion that slavery should be abolished or even questioned.

Although humans typically look upon anyone different than themselves with fear, disdain, trepidation, contempt or admonition, skin color was not a factor in who was or wasn't a slave until fairly recent times, primarily the discovery of the New World and its need for cheap labor forcibly imported from Africa. African slaves, numbering in the millions, soon became near majorities in many areas of plantation-style single crop and mining economies primarily located in South America, the Caribbean and the southern United States. In these areas, black skin meant slave status and vice-versa, but this was almost unique in world history. The vast majority of slaves in the world were of every color, every gene pool, and every cultural archetype of all peoples everywhere.

While it is true people who were different than those holding power were disproportionately slaves, skin color generally had little to do with this. Slaves were often the conquered people (the Hittites were slaves to the conquering Egyptians), the recent unwanted immigrants (the Jews in Babylon), those without land (the Gypsies in Hungary), those who spoke and dressed differently (The Burmese in Siam), those of 'inferior blood' (the Slavs and Jews in Nazi Germany), those born into it ('bred' slaves made up most of the slave population in Third Century Rome), or those who couldn't support themselves in any other way (serfs selling themselves into slavery in 18th Century Russia). A 'slave race' of dark-skinned people like in the southern United States in the 19th century, mainly born into it by that time and reproducing itself with considerable gain generation after generation, is an unparalleled event in world history.

Moving from slave to free status varies drastically from culture to culture, but usually it takes three full generations to gain full free status devoid of residual prejudice. In Ancient Rome a slave could be manumitted to become a freedman who still bore many obligations to his former owner, but his children would in fact be free and eligible for citizenship. In the inside passage of Alaska grandchildren of former slaves still bear the burden of the social stigma of 'coming from slaves.' In many Middle Eastern countries the word 'abn' in your name tells the world your parents had at one time been property of others. Certainly in the United States slave status was maintained long after federal abolition through so-called "Jim Crow" laws with both social and legal segregation based on slave-skin color designations.

Although the word slavery has many meanings and denotes various shades of ownership/control that vary from culture to culture, it is safe to say the word clearly indicates an individual has lost many choices concerning his life as compared to 'free' peoples. At its most severe, slavery is 'chattel slavery' i.e., you are the pure property of whoever owns you as much as a cow or a horse - you are human livestock with no more rights or privileges than a pig bought at market. But even in milder forms, slaves generally cannot choose what work they do or where they do it; they have obligations, social and economic, to those who have rights over them; they cannot develop or advance themselves without their owner's permission; and usually are restricted as to who they can mate with, the control they have over their offspring, and the benefits they can enjoy from their own labor.

Slavery is alive and well today, although many efforts are made to suppress this knowledge. Some experts claim there are over 21 million bonafide slaves in the 21st century although how they arrive at this figure is questionable. Much of this is so-called 'economic slavery' - generational debt management keeps a people bound to a specific job at a specific place (Indian land debt is probably the best example of this). Other contemporary slavery is economic manipulation of illegal immigrants who are held in bondage due to immigration laws, unscrupulous 'job placement managers,' etc. For example, many clothing articles in today's world are made by people who are legally stateless, paid next to nothing, housed in shabby barracks, and fed a mere subsistence diet. Household servants in the oil-rich countries of the Middle East are another example. Still others, usually those young and attractive, are forced into sexual slavery, placed in situations where allowing sexual usage of their body is the only way to stay alive, e.g., prostitutes in Sri Lanka and Thailand. Like slaves for thousands of years before them, these contemporary slaves are of every color, every ethnic and religious background and every national origin. What they have in common with their forbearers are their powerlessness, their alienated social status, and their perceived lack of any viable alternatives.

Lastly, slaves did and still do practically any human activity ever known. But primarily slaves were and are utilized to do what free people don't want to do: tasks requiring huge amounts of fatiguing, backbreaking labor (like quarry work or mining); tasks that are extremely unpleasant (like working with sewage or tanning leather); tasks that are socially humiliating (like being 'put down' in public or doing acts that free people refuse to perform); or tasks that demand a denial of self-respect (like prostitution). Consequently, you rarely find slaves in socially prestigious positions, slaves in positions which they might choose themselves, or slaves in positions that lead to social advancement. Humans all too often take advantage of opportunities to 'lord it over' others, 'put others down,' or enjoy telling others what to do. In its most extreme, you can use another's body to bring you sensual pleasures without any consensual concerns. In this respect slavery offers a ready, convenient, and legal outlet for these human passions.

The wonder is that most civilized societies managed to get rid of legitimate slavery, no matter how recent. The fact that what slavery remains is underground and generally illegal is one of the greatest accomplishments of human history and certainly the crowning achievement of human rights overall.

CONTEMPORARY INTEREST IN SLAVERY

During the past 20 years, there has been a renaissance of interest in the practice of slavery. In part this is because considerable new information has become available about historical slaves and their conditions. Perhaps it is because illegal (and usually hidden) contemporary slavery has reappeared globally, some estimating the number in the millions.

Perhaps it is because we just can't understand why millions and millions of people had allowed others to exploit them so totally. Why didn't slaves rebel? Usually they significantly outnumbered their overseers and owners combined. And how could they allow such a degree of exploitation, humiliation, shame, and manipulation? Most contemporaries have trouble understanding how people allowed themselves to be led around like sheep, so to speak, doing all the things others didn't want to do themselves. For example, scholars have written many articles asking why the Jews held as literal slaves by the Nazi Germans in World War II and slated for extermination didn't rebel since they outnumbered their executors many times over. Why do contemporary illegal slaves, who are forced into activities they abhor (like prostitution) not simply refuse or walk away from their 'owners'? Why did some historical slaves tolerate assignments that had little work contribution but were simply pleasure contributions to their owners, such as concubinage, display objects, or objects to enhance their owner's prestige? Why did some highly educated Greeks, trained in the classics, in medicine, in music, etc., allow themselves to be chattel slaves to owners who had none of their talents or skills? Many of these questions are perplexing and history books typically offer few answers to these questions if they address them at all.

Others compare slavery to employment in a job they don't like. But there's a huge difference between being an employee and being a slave, even if both do the same task. An employee gets direct benefits and can choose to quit. A slave usually gets no direct benefits and has no choice as to whether they do the activity or not. Furthermore, slavery was often a hereditary condition, totally unlike being an employee (no matter how exploited or manipulated that employee may feel). Few employees were ever denied quitting and moving on, an option never allowed slaves. So that comparison doesn't stand up.

The comparison between government prisoners and slaves isn't totally fruitful either. Prisoners are interned as punishment - that's often not true in the case of slaves who can be born into slavery. And prisoners are notoriously bad workers - so much so that we don't even bother much anymore trying to get them to do serious work. The effort of getting them to work is often more trouble than it's worth. The status of prisoner is never heritable. A prisoner, in the worst possible scenario, can be put to death but his or her children aren't incarcerated or punished directly. In contrast, contemporary Indian 'debt slaves' paying back their debt to a landowner through assigned labor pass the debt labor onto their children who can pass it onto their children generation after generation.

Some point to drug addiction as another form of slavery emerging in contemporary society wherein the addict is often a 'slave' to the supplier and forced into prostitution, thievery, embezzlement, domestic chores, selling the drug themselves, etc., in order to maintain an insured supply for themselves. But this is not chattel slavery in that the supplier doesn't actually own the person and has no legal rights over him or her despite their strong hold on that person's actions.

Sociologists point out that people always seem willing to exploit other people, if given half a chance, and so we must safeguard against giving people any opportunities or expectations in that area. They also point out that people all too often won't work if they can find a way for other people to do it for them. Psychologists point out that the ability to have total control over people almost always leads to sexual exploitation of one type or another if the owned are sexually attractive to the owner. Psychologists also point out that actually owning a person body and soul almost invariably tends to bring out our worst exploitative motives.

When Americans think of slavery, they think of the Ancient Romans (primarily due to some popular movies like *Gladiator, Ben Hur, The Robe,* and *Quo Vadis*) or the American South prior to the Civil War.

Roman slavery was characterized by its longevity (over 1000 years), its scope (most of the known world at that time), its extent (huge numbers of the populace were enslaved at any given time), its cruelty (disobedience usually led to death) and its utilization of slaves in professional and managerial roles (physicians, educators, accountants, etc.).

Slavery in the United States was relatively brief (300-400 years), was uniquely race-related, was the only slave society where natural reproduction of slaves kept steadily increasing thereby eliminating the need for the imports of new slaves (which was restricted by Congress in 1820), and was only eliminated in 1865. It also had more legislation concerning slaves and limitations on slave behavior than any country up to that time.

But many other societies practiced slavery on a large scale also. Notable was Korea in the late eighteenth century (which had one of the largest slave societies ever known outside the Romans); Russia in the early nineteenth century (which was unique in that serfs frequently sold themselves into slavery to better their condition); Sweden in the mid-sixteenth century where slavery (called thralldom there) was widely practiced and was particularly brutish and harsh; or France or Germany in the eleventh century where so many Slavs were enslaved, we changed the word 'servi' meaning an owned chattel to 'slave,' since Slav and slave were synonymous for a century or two.

FOUR PREDOMINANT MYTHS
SURROUNDING SLAVERY

There are many myths surrounding the history of slavery. Some are the result of deliberate distortions on the part of religionists; some are the result of poor scholarship or taking the plight of slaves out of their cultural context; some are the result of abolitionists' zeal who sometimes overlooked the reality of slavery in their efforts to get rid of it entirely.

Perhaps the most prevalent myth in the Western world is that Christianity brought an end to the practice of slavery (at least legally). While it is true that in the 18th and 19th centuries a good number of Christian ministers in England and in the New England areas of the United States denounced the practice of slavery most vehemently and that the 'abolitionist' movements in both England and the United States were often associated with various Christian organizations, there were an equal number of Christian leaders during that same time who supported slavery as an institution, even pointing out numerous Biblical passages to support their position.

Anti or pro-slavery Christian proscriptions seemed to be based more on geography than a given Christian position: English, Canadian and Northern U.S. religious leaders proclaimed God's will was strongly against slavery (i.e., it was wrong for one human to own another in that all men are equal in God's eye); Southern U.S. and South American religions leaders just as zealously proclaimed God ordained slavery with definite purposes in mind (i.e., blacks were, by God's will, innately inferior intellectually and morally and needed the structure and guidance slavery offered them).

The abolitionist position conveniently overlooks that God apparently had changed his mind over time in that unequal status among men was tolerated in God's world for tens of centuries before, including writing in the U.S. Declaration of Independence that "all men are created equal" unless, of course, you were a slave where you didn't count at all as a 'man'. It also overlooks that the Roman Catholic church condoned massive imported black and indigenous native slavery in the New World as long as the slaves themselves were blessed by a priest and their owners promised to make some attempt to convert them to Christian beliefs prior to their being worked to death. Stretching all logic to the point of absurdity is the description of Catholic priests 'converting' thousands of natives forced off their own land, enchained into forced labor, and working under the whip of their foreign masters presumably headed toward a better life in Heaven now that they had been properly baptized into an alien faith. But this may not seem too illogical when you realize that slavery was widespread in Europe up until it was replaced with serfdom around 1000 A.D. or so and that the Catholic church itself was the single largest slaveholder in all of Europe at that time. Apparently, Christianity as practiced for almost two thousand years could accommodate the institution of slavery with no qualms whatsoever. The Reform Movement (Protestantism) didn't place the practice of slavery on its moral agenda either. It simply isn't mentioned as part of the protest against Catholic practices at that time. Indeed, Protestants involved in the colonial expansion of the 17th and 18th centuries embraced black slavery with zeal as the God-given answer to their plantation labor needs (although they mainly saw no need to make concerted efforts to convert the black slaves to their own belief systems like the Catholics did, outside of using the practice of religion as yet another way to control slaves).

Another 'myth' concerning slavery is that most slaves accepted their status with little objection. Slaves born into slavery were generally more docile in their acceptance, knowing nothing else but a slave's life since birth. Being forcibly transferred from free status to slave status was often another matter entirely and such persons usually had to be chained, beaten and starved into subjection. Historians point out that there were actually few slave revolts considering the thousands of years of slavery and the millions enslaved. Most persons have read about the Roman Servile War and its leader of the revolting slaves, the gladiator Spartacus. Fewer are familiar with the two major revolts of slaves in Sicily earlier. All three of these major slave revolts in ancient times ended with massive executions of the slaves involved, e.g., the Roman Servile War ended with 6000 slaves crucified on crosses (one of the most painful deaths imaginable) lining the Appian Way for over 50 miles. Prior to that, a minor slave revolt in the city of Rome itself led to over 200 slaves being coated with pitch and burned alive in a public field as an example to all other slaves who might have harbored some thoughts about escape from their bondage. In the United States centuries later, runaway or rebelling slaves usually were punished with loss of legs, ears, or sexual organs. In Spain rebelling slaves as late as the 18th century were punished by cutting their leg tendons, their tongues, or face branding. The list could go on and on.

Usually, reactions toward slaves who didn't accept their servile status in almost any fashion were swift and fierce. The action was designed to instill so much fear in a slave that even the thought of rebellion became unthinkable. Consequently most punishments for not accepting slavery were, if not a painful death, bodily mutilation and/or disfigurement, and almost always staged publicly so the consequences of such action became a model for other slaves to ponder. Such actions did work, no matter how barbaric, and simply proves that fear is one of humans' most powerful motives to conform to the expected social role.

It should be noted that everywhere slavery was practiced, the first thing established was a legal code outlining ownership rights of a master over his slaves, the establishment of slaves as property distinguishing them from all other humans, and in the most extreme cases classifying them as a separate species more like animals than humans. Hence, Romans sometimes referred to their slaves as 'talking animals' (dictio grex) or 'speaking livestock'. Legal codes also prescribed appropriate slave behavior with legalized and required punishment for deviancy from these 'slave codes'. At its most absurd slave suicide was defined as theft of an owner's property with the punishment to be mutilation of an already dead slave's corpse. Running away from your owner was likewise seen legally as theft of your owner's property and consequently was treated the same as a slave actually stealing material goods from his master or mistress. Most legal codes also viewed a slave's body as property of his owner with the master or mistress having full rights over that body and anything produced by that body including all labor that could be extracted from that body, offspring produced by the slave's body, and even sexual pleasures that could be extracted from the slave's body.

Although physical fear certainly kept most slaves in line, the legal code guaranteed there were no alternatives to a slave from his proscribed life. One wag has noted 'where there are slaves, there is also the whip' which is a nice way of saying the chronic possibility of severe physical pain was always present in a slave's life. Beatings, starvation, branding, shackling, and execution were ever-present in a slave's life whether it was in Ancient Rome, Korea, Russia, Siam or Brazil.

Psychological fear also reinforced a slave's conformity to his social role. There was always the fear of being sold off to a worst plight (usually the mines or galleys), the fear of reduced rations, the fear of public shaming, the fear of getting sick or old and being abandoned, the fear of having your children sold off to unknown places, the fear of being forced to be publicly naked, the fear of sexual exploitation, and numerous other methods of keeping people working diligently under the direction of others.

Considering that all of these 'control factors' were well in place, it is a wonder that any slaves ever revolted. Nevertheless, occasionally they did but the success rate was practically nil.

A third 'myth' is that the vast majority of slaves were contented and happy in their bondage - the picture of the happy, smiling slaves in America's Currier and Ives prints comes to mind. The idea presented was that slaves were by nature 'childlike', were happiest in situations where personal choices were limited, and where someone else took care of their needs. Nowhere was this picture of slavery more zealously presented than in the American South in the early 19th century. Ministers preached that black slaves were morally deficient and needed the 'guidance' of Christian beliefs; economists argued that black slaves were inherently lazy and needed strong motivation (mainly a good whip) to work up to their potential; and educators argued that blacks were inherently inferior in mental capacity and it was a waste of time to educate them beyond simple manual skills. This myth was so prevalent that even the black slaves bought into it, e.g.,the black educator Booker T. Washington proposed blacks should initially be taught only manual trades in that they were incapable at this point in their development of more intellectually challenging topics. Believing this, white masters often decided what religious beliefs were appropriate for a simple mind; what tasks should be taught a black slave; that formal education was a waste of time and even 'dangerous'; and that it was best if the master decided who and when they should mate with even if a formal marriage was denied slaves.

But interviews with ex-slaves following the Civil War revealed anything but a happy, contented population of black slaves. Slaves frequently tried to secretly sabotage some of their owner's projects, longed to learn to read if given half a chance, deeply resented forced mating, and perhaps most of all resented the fact they were isolated to their owner's property and often denied any relief from the monotony of doing the same tasks day after day in the same location. As one ex-slave put it "what I wanted most of all was to see what was going on beyond Master _____'s plantation - I wanted to see a town or some other women or even some other slaves for a change." The redundancy of most slave's lives, especially agricultural and mining slaves, cannot be overstated and was at best a thorough dulling of a human's spirit.

Perhaps the biggest resentment of all was that many slaves were treated like other bought livestock (cattle, horses, etc). They were bought solely to make a profit for their owners, were often treated with minimum food and shelter like other livestock, sometimes deliberately bred to produce more sellable slaves, and worse of all, they knew their owners often thought of them as merely another form of animal.

A fourth 'myth' is that human society works best with a well-controlled substrata of submissives similar to that seen in the 'natural' animal world. For example, bee colonies have their 'worker' bees that resemble slaves in that they do most of the work, supporting an upperclass 'queen' and her court and ants also have workers and commanders designated by birth status which resemble slaves and masters in the human world.

The Greek philosopher Plato intellectualized slave status among humans when he stated in his *Republic* that nature always had a submissive class balanced by a dominant class: slaves were 'born' to be submissive; masters were 'born' to guide them. This was true even for those enslaved later in their life (i.e., not born into their servile status). The 'fate' decided by the gods had led to them being enslaved - it was the slave's role to embrace his fate, learn to live with it, and find what happiness and satisfaction he or she could within their servile status. Aristotle expanded this position: in his *Politics* he states: "for that some should rule and others be ruled is a thing not only necessary, but expedient; from the hour of their birth, some are marked out for subjection, others for rule." Those 'marked out for subjection' were the slaves of course. Plato's and Aristotle's thinking predominated Western thought for the next 17 to 18 centuries and lead to a highly structured class society in most Western civilizations - all part of the natural order of things and part of a divine plan. This convenient 'excuse' for human slavery originated in what we now call 'The Cradle of Democracy' but the democratic ideology espoused always had its foundation firmly in a subclass of slaves who were denied any freedoms whatsoever.

The most prominent religions slaves were exposed to reinforced Aristotle's and Plato's concepts of life satisfaction being most related to personal acceptance of the gods' (or God's) fate. If you were enslaved accept it as your destiny and try to find happiness within your bondage. If you were born into slavery that fate in and of itself wouldn't have happened if it wasn't part of your fate. In either case, recently enslaved or born into slavery, to be anything other than a slave would be defying the gods and would certainly bring unhappiness and personal grief in the long run. Many slaves accepted this inwardly and lived out their servile lives with little thought of trying to change their personal fate. Many masters accepted this also and saw their domination over others as a natural right, if not duty. The end result was many slaves never fought against their almost total lack of freedom in living their lives; many masters never gave a thought as to the consequences of their commands on their slaves' lives - indeed, numerous masters publicly complained about the overwhelming burden of supervising their slaves' lives.

The legal codes in most slave societies reflected the predominant religions of that society and set down the restrictions and obligations of both slave and master. Therefore, both those owned and their owners rarely ventured much thought about slavery over and beyond the prevailing dictums of the day. A slave would have to be rebellious beyond belief to question the legal/moral pillars of his world. Similarly, a slave owner would have to be heretical to question his ownership of other humans, especially if those humans owned were certainly below him in almost all respects, if not indeed animalistic in nature.

Slaves were widely, but not universally, seen as a subspecies of humans, little different than other domestic animals. Like other animals they responded well to the whip, but they had the advantage of human speech and faster learning than most other animals (although Romans generally agreed horses on the average were easier to train than slaves). Biologically, slaves were generally viewed as less delicate than other humans - they were more enduring in hard physical labor, for instance, and were almost devoid of most emotional aspects of humans such as grief, romantic love, sorrow, joy, or strong familial ties. Slaves felt less physical pain than non-slaves. Hence, brandings, burning, severe beatings, etc., were less traumatic to a slave and led to their quick recovery from such events. Sex among slaves was animalistic and didn't involve any aspects of romantic love; grief was almost impossible in that slaves were incapable of strong love to start with; and family life was relatively meaningless to a slave who had no legal rights to marriage, legitimate birth, inheritance, or the right to own property. The fact that a slave could be sold upon the whim of her or his owner to any destiny with no consultation on the part of the person being sold probably told a slave where he stood in this life more than anything else that happened to her or him. The adage 'treat a person like an animal and they will become one' may have been proven true in the case of many slaves.

Types Of Slaves

Most slaves in the world were **chattel slaves**, i.e., they were the property of whoever bought them and were no different than any other owned property (cows, horses, land, etc.). Such slaves had no individual rights whatsoever, no restrictions as to their sale or to whom, and could be put to any tasks, no matter how onerous. Chattel slaves could be put to death upon the wish of their owner, punished in any matter, have their body altered or mutilated to their owner's desires, be forcibly mated for reproductive purposes, or used sexually for the pleasure of their owner. They were 'outside' normal laws, including legal marriage, rights to their offspring, or protection of civil laws inherent in the society in which they had been sold. Usually slaveholding societies had an elaborate legal code regulating the sale, transfer, control, and appropriate punishment for deviations from the expected behavior of chattel slaves. Almost all legal codes specified minimum punishments for such chattel behavior as running away, hitting a free man, destroying an owner's property (including him or herself), refusing a master or mistress' command, talking back to their master, showing disrespect for their mistress or master, unauthorized mating or other sexual activities, stealing, etc. Such 'slave codes' date back to the Sumerians in 3000 B.C., are part of I Iammurabi's Code in ancient Babylonia (1800 B.C.), can be found in the Old Testament, are elaborately spelled out in Roman law (300 B.C. - 400 A.D.), and reach their most codification in legislation passed in the American South during the 18th and 19th century. During this latter period, specific punishments were legalized for slaves learning to read, masters attempting to teach a slave to read, slaves not lowering their eyes in the presence of a white person, miscegenation (cohabitation between persons of different races) or anyone, slave or free, 'spreading unauthorized religious or abolitionist thoughts'.

Chattel slavery was much preferred because it gave the slaveholder unlimited rights over his bought property and was the least complicated for the slaveholding society to deal with - as property slaves invariably found themselves at the very bottom of social status and, having no civil rights, were easy to deal with legally - the slave owner was responsible for the slave's behavior in all regards. Hence a slave committing murder often led to a fine imposed on the owner (for not controlling the slave better) as well as the slave's tortuous death - both required by the legal code. A slave stealing goods belonging to someone not his owner required the slave's owner to recompense the victim. Perhaps the most complicated was where a male slave impregnated a female slave belonging to another person without the express permission of both owners. The offspring belonged to the owner of the female slave in that any issuance from a slave's womb belonged to that slave's owner, but if the pregnancy was unwanted, did the owner of the male slave owe recompense for the 'damage' done to the female slave? Even the Hammurabi Code tackled such issues and many more and in the process becomes an interesting listing of social problems inherent in almost any society.

Slavery with restrictions was practiced within some societies however and the restrictions allowed varied widely from one geographic region to another. In certain parts of Africa, for example, slaves were given the right to marry, to live with their partner and their offspring (all remaining slaves), and could not be sold off outside their tribal origins. In still other areas, slavery was not necessarily for life, but had time/ duty restrictions, e.g., slavery for 30 years only; slavery until certain government projects were completed, or slavery until sufficient captives were obtained so that native slaves were no longer needed. Such slaves were still considered legitimate property of their owners and are sometimes referred to as **quasi-chattel slaves**, but slaves they were.

Some whole tribes were considered 'slave tribes' subject to their overlords and anyone in that tribe or born into it were slaves by nature of their birth. The Tuaregs of Central Africa were most noted as inherent slave masters over neighboring tribes for centuries and in Southwest

Africa the Hottentots were considered a 'slave' tribe by other tribes surrounding them for thousands of years, ripe for harvesting as slaves whenever needed. Perhaps the strangest arrangement was in the area now occupied by modern Mauritania where African blacks are considered the 'natural' slaves of Arab masters, an arrangement dating back at least a thousand years and which, unfortunately, is still going on according to many news reports. Mauritanian slavery is unique in another aspect also. Any product of a male slave's sperm is considered a slave, despite the mother's status. Hence, free women can produce slaves as well as slave women, but just how this is determined puzzles many outside observers.

Serfdom eventually replaced slavery in most of Europe and large parts of Asia. The transition of slaves to serfs to peasants took well over a thousand years and was gradual. Europe, for example, still had many chattel slaves being bought and sold in open markets around 1000 A.D., although they were outnumbered by serfs by that time. Serfs, unlike slaves, could not be bought and sold on open markets to just anyone. They were restricted to work the land of their lord, usually the same land they were born on. They could not move to another lord's land, they could farm for themselves at their own pace and schedule, but they had to give (generally one-third) to the landowner who in turn provided them protection from 'capture or killing' by outside forces. The lord was not responsible for preventing their starvation in bad years, but it was in his long-term economic interest to do so. It was 'share-cropping' on a massive scale where a small minority owned almost all the land. Serfs could not own land themselves, their offspring were obligated to work the land of their parents and they were obligated to do other chores (such as building a castle) as specified by their lord. The lord also had sexual rights over the first born daughter if he so desired. The transition of the Roman world to the serfdom of medieval Europe was prolonged. For example, as late as 480 A.D. the will of a Roman widow 'freed' over 20,000 slaves into 'obligated servants', i.e., serfs. Nowhere was the number of serfs greater than in 15th-19th century Russia where they were kept in miserable conditions by absentee landlords - conditions so bad many voluntarily sold themselves into chattel slavery simply to escape starvation. Eventually serfs gained a few more rights outside of land ownership, and became essentially tenant farmers called **peasants**

within most societies. Eighteenth century Europe and Russia was mainly filled with peasants, not serfs. Asian countries at this time, however, lagged behind and still practiced massive slavery, with some serfs. The Middle East remained primarily slave societies until the middle of the 20th century.

Sources Of Slaves

Originally prisoners of war were simply killed. But dead bodies can't 'pay back' the costs of war, and enslavement replaced execution so the labor their bodies could produce was utilized for the conqueror's benefit, both in public works as well as the capital private sales yielded. This transition was seen as 'merciful' in that the losing side was spared, albeit slaves for life. Such prisoners were the main source of slaves for ancient civilizations and probably reached its peak at the time of the Roman Empire where human booty from foreign lands flooded the slave markets - so much so that slave prices dropped dramatically. Slave merchants (actually corporate slave brokers) followed the Roman armies, giving the army immediate cash for their prisoners and then efficiently shipping these captives to the massive slave transshipment center located on the island of Delos, the huge slave markets of Rome and Alexandria and the smaller slave markets in all other large cities sprinkled throughout the Empire. This transfer of human captives was a huge industry, extremely profitable, and well organized. For those captured it usually meant being shipped to an alien culture where they couldn't understand the language, losing all sources of social support, and suddenly finding themselves regarded as property rather than a fellow human being.

But wars eventually end and the ready supply of slaves from conquest decreases. Prices of slaves go up due to their decreasing numbers and at some point raising slaves from birth becomes profitable. Since universally the product of a slave womb was automatically a slave him or herself, natural reproduction of the slave population offered a steady supply of new slaves to the market. But such slaves had to bring enough at auction to offset the costs of raising them from birth to a marketable age and in periods of extensive conquest, their prices were often not competitive with fresh captives.

During such times owners discouraged slave reproduction by various means. Many male slaves were placed in sex-segregated situations (such as mines, quarries, and galleys) where reproduction simply wasn't possible; even where both sexes of slaves worked together (such as in farming or factories), opportunities for mating were highly restricted; or, at its most extreme, pregnancies were forcibly aborted, slave newborns were abandoned to the elements (called 'exposure' where they usually quickly died unless promptly picked up by an adult willing to rear the child until he could be sold at market), or male slaves were castrated so the expense of raising slaves from birth to market could be avoided.

However, bred slaves usually had a market premium in that slave training and adjustment was generally already accomplished by the time the slave was first sold at auction and were considered less troublesome by most buyers in that such slaves knew no existence outside of slavery. Therefore, when captive slaves became scarce and prices rose, natural reproduction of the slave population was strongly encouraged. Although slaves could not legally marry, opportunities for cohabitation were provided and factors effecting higher reproduction rates were employed such as proper rest to prevent exhaustion, proper diet to prevent malnutrition, praise and other rewards for the production of children (even to the point of promising manumission for slave mothers producing 10 or more children in at least one instance), allowing slave families to stay together until children were of marketable age, and considerably easier work assignments for pregnant slaves. The most dramatic example of encouraging slave reproduction was in the American South following passage of a law in 1820 prohibiting further import of foreign slaves. Within a generation slaves were reproducing themselves many times over, creating a dramatic increase in the number of available slaves despite the ban on import of new slaves. Since written records are available for this period, it appears increases in both quantity and quality of food provided the slaves, decreased work loads to prevent physical exhaustion, allowance of family life among slaves, and providing incentives for new births (such as money, privileges, promises of eventual manumission, etc.) led rather quickly to marked increases in slave reproduction. (In fact, the American South seems to be the only slave-holding culture that managed to dramatically increase natural reproduction rates among their slave population.)

Despite this, slave mothers in many cultures sometimes tried to abort their fetuses or killed their own offspring at birth in efforts to prevent their progeny from ending up being sold as slaves like their parent. Likewise male slaves sometimes did what they could to prevent impregnating their companions for the same purpose.

Piracy, kidnapping, and retrieval of exposed infants were other sources of slaves although relatively minor compared to the enslavement of war captives and natural reproduction of the existing slave population. Like war captives, persons simply stolen for the slave markets were cheap to obtain, offered huge profits, but could prove cantankerous in adjusting to their new status and had the added problem of family members trying to reclaim them if they could be located. Retrieving 'exposed' infants to be raised as slaves incurred the costs of raising a child to the point where he would be worth anything (in periods of slave surpluses, slave children brought close to nothing at most markets due to the costs of raising them to the stage where they would be productive). Exposure was the usual fate of any child born malformed or suffering some visible birth defect regardless of its origins, free or slave during most of ancient times - the chances of such children being rescued was probably slight in that they would have little market value when of sellable age.

There were other sources of slaves. Courts could sentence people into full chattel slavery for crimes ranging from murder to theft to indebtedness, thus producing an enslaved native population that was already trained for local conditions (language, skills, social expectations of slaves, etc.). Both France and Great Britain practiced this rather extensively in their early history, thereby producing large number of native-born slaves for their early colonial labor needs. (France utilized prisoners as galley slaves right up until the 18th century.) Ancient Rome practiced this rather extensively, thereby saving the cost of imprisoning their citizens. As slaves became scarcer, the laws allowing enslavement tended to become more liberal so that the slave supply from this source increased. Some of these court-sentenced enslavements were for specified periods of time, distinguishing them from the usual type of life-time slavery and were a precursor of our modern court system in this regard.

Some societies allowed self-enslavement where a person could escape his/her debtors, unemployment, family problems, pending court sentencing, or most likely, starvation, through the act of offering himself for sale - either for a lifetime or, more commonly, for a specified period. Imperial Russia probably had the highest rate of permanent self-enslavement, mainly as a means of escaping starvation as a peasant. Sometimes, especially in Arab countries, persons could pick their own master, specify restrictions as to their usage, guarantee access to their family, or gain prohibitions about being resold as part of the enslavement process. In the Americas following the early 1800s a white was prohibited from selling himself into slavery (the institution was legally reserved for blacks only by that time).

There are few historically creditable accounts of selectively breeding slaves which resembled that widely practiced in the animal world of horses, cows, pigs, dogs, etc. The advantages of eugenics (human selective breeding) was understood by slave holders and chattel slavery gave them the legal right to control slave reproduction any way they saw fit. But the implementation of selectively breeding humans proved extremely difficult. Slaves deeply resented being bred like animals and sabotaged the results whenever possible. Restricting slaves to specific partners proved difficult and slaves often refused to participate, regardless of the punishments such action might incur. Unlike animals, slaves could think out the consequences of their actions and would not participate in the production of a superior strain of new slaves.

The most notable exception to the failure of these eugenics schemes (although not involving slaves) was the 'love gardens' of Nazi Germany in which highly select SS officers were selectively mated with the best of the women in the Hitler Youth Movement to produce a 'super-race' of pure Aryans superior in intelligence, physique, disease resistance, and so-called Aryan characteristics of blond hair and blue eyes. Although the project only lasted three years until the collapse of Germany, thousands of babies were produced who ultimately were placed in foster homes throughout post-war Germany. Follow-up studies revealed the project had been successful in that, on the average, the babies were above average in intelligence, physique, and disease resistance although, with the movement away from the Nazi Aryan superiority philosophy, they carried the burden of the social shame of their origins. Nowadays, with implanted embryos, sperm storage, in vitro fertilization, etc., techniques well developed, selective breeding among a slave population might be an entirely different story. Indeed, given totalitarian control, the development of a specific 'slave race' might indeed be possible over several generations.

Physical, Psychological & Social Control Of Slaves

The most obvious form of slave control was physical: shackles that limited bodily movement; chains that bound them to each other or to rungs in walls, etc.; collars that forced their heads into upright positions; harnesses that attached them to plows, wagons, etc.; and cages and cells that contained them at night.

When a person was first enslaved almost all of these were routinely used (and probably necessary) to prevent rebellion or flight. Wrists and ankles were often permanently banded so that restraining chains could be easily attached as needed, although some owners used such bands merely as decoration on their slaves or as a denotation of their slave status. Similarly, permanent collars had several uses: (1) you could leash a slave to others or to a ring in a wall or other stationary object easily by a corresponding ring attached to a collar, offering a foolproof way to keep a slave in place; (2) you could identify the slave's owner and identification number by simply engraving it into the collar; (3) it served to clearly identify the person so collared as an owned object so there was no confusion as to his/her status; and (4) perhaps most important, it constantly reminded the collared person himself that he or she was similar to other domestic animals similarly collared.

Other physical devices were also used to identity slaves: clipping ears denoted not only slave status but often a particular owner by the type of cut employed; brands on the face, neck, cheek, arms, chest or buttocks denoted slave status and usually identified the slave's owner;

rarely, rings through the nose were used as slave decorations, similar to control rings placed through other animal noses such as oxen or pigs. In later times (Nazi Germany, for example) tattoos were placed on forearms or foreheads to identify and codify slaves by unique numbers.

Of all these body markings branding was by far the most common throughout the ages: it was permanent (brand scars are practically impossible to remove), it clearly denoted slave status, and it was widely believed branding was essential for a person to realize he was now the property of someone else and that an owner's mark now was a permanent part of him. Also, many slave dealers thought branding, since it was extremely painful (usually a person loses consciousness in the process as well as loses all bodily control) demonstrated to a slave better than any other means that he was subject to his master's will in all aspects. (For example, Roman slave dealers reportedly had the slogan: "A good branding saves a thousand whippings.")

Outside of branding which was usually a one-time occurrence (unless subsequent owners added their own 'mark'), many of these physical control devices were mainly used when first enslaving a person and or in the process of 'breaking' them to their new status. Once acclimated to his slavery, many of these devices were removed in that they were no longer needed (such as shackles, arm, wrist, and ankle bands), although some owners (particularly Romans) kept collars on their slaves permanently.

Slaves could usually be identified by other physical means outside of restraint and control devices. Dress provided slaves were often exclusive to the slave population, e.g., Roman slaves usually were issued short tunics. Specified haircuts (usually very short hair such as U.S. Marines wear during their training) were often required of all slaves as a means of identification, along with unique earrings worn only by slaves, neck pendants announcing they were the property of a particular house or plantation, and sometimes unique headbands told the world their slave status. Usually slaves were easily identified by their shabby or hand-me-down clothing, their owner's specified livery, or, in the most humiliating of cases, given no clothes to wear at all (not that uncommon among galley and mining slaves during the Roman period where clothing was seen as a waste of money).

Physical control was usually visible and was obviously effective in restraining movement as well as making slaves easily distinguished from the population at large.

But psychological control of slaves was probably even more effective in getting a slave to do what his master or mistress wanted. Fear of physical punishment was so effective that many owners (and dealers) exposed a new slave to horrible beatings initially so that fear was internalized rather permanently. Therefore, slave-owners usually dealt out punishment for disobedience swiftly, savagely, and publicly where all his other slaves could witness the consequences of even the hint of not complying with their master's wishes. Sometimes these physical punishments (often beatings with a variety of whips designed for the purpose) were so horrific the slave died as a result. If they lived through the ordeal their backs were often permanently scarred as a reminder to all who saw them of the price of disobedience. Leg tendons were sometimes cut if a slave tried to run away so the slave was forced to crawl from then on; tongues were ripped out for talking back to a master or of complaining to others; hands were cut off for stealing the master's or other's property; hot brands were applied to those not working hard enough if the whips weren't thought effective; and, if all else failed to shape a slave into acceptance of his lot, food and sleep deprivation were used, along with extra work assignments although these later punishments risked loss of the slave they were trying to discipline. All of these elements of physical pain produced dread of future punishment - a very powerful psychological determinant of subsequent behavior. So fear was in the back of every slave's mind and probably accounts for the submissive acquiescence to an owner's commands typically seen in slaves over many, many centuries.

Psychological controls went far beyond fear, however. Most slaves lost their adult status with their induction into slavery. Suddenly they were referred to as 'boys' rather than men and indeed were often called nothing else. The Roman word for boy 'puer' became the most common label for slaves of any age in that time as it did in the American South for black slaves who answered to the term 'boy' more often than in response to their given slave name. This language manipulation was deliberate: it moved the slave down to the dependent status of a child and was a constant reminder to the slave him or herself that they were in fact dependent on their owner for their very lives. Similarly, most slaves were renamed at the time of their sale (including subsequent sales) by their new owner dependent on the owner's inclinations. Romans liked to name their slaves unique slave names, like 'Rufus' similar to the way we name dogs or cats unique names, such as 'Spot' or 'Tabby.' Asians tended to name slaves after their assigned function, like 'Well-Digger' or 'Runner'. Masters in the American South tended to prefer names from Greek mythology, like 'Xerxes' or 'Agamemnon'. A new name decided by your owner demonstrated several things: (1) it told the slave his owner could call his new possession anything he liked; (2) it signified the slave's old pre-slave life, including that 'free' name, was now gone; (3) the name was usually derogatory in that it demoted a slave to dependent, child-like status and the new name usually was unique to slaves, therefore not only identifying him or her as a slave to the society at large, but also constantly reminding her or him he was a slave. When an owner announced he would now call his new possession a certain name and the slave was to forget whatever he was called before, it clearly established that master had the right to do so and what the slave thought about losing a good part of his personal identity had no consequence whatsoever.

The fact a collar around his neck was identical to collars used on other animals (especially pets) was not lost on the slave. It told the world at large he was a possession of others, especially when the collar often identified his owner and sometimes included a reward notice for return of the collared slave. Collars were problematic for those wearing them: if your neck size increased with increased muscle growth or fat, breathing could be restricted; collars too loose often caused abrasions and sores around the neck; collars too tall restricted the slave's ability to lower his head for any reason. But worst of all, a collar denoted animal status in that only animals were fitted with them.

Specified slave clothes or an owner's livery eliminated any possibility of individuality being expressed by the slave. Much like hired help today in restaurants usually wearing a t-shirt with the company's logo on it which identifies them as an employee, slaves wore livery announcing they belonged to a certain house, a certain farm or plantation, a certain corporation, etc. The difference is that hired help can dress anyway they want once they are 'off-duty' and usually doff those specified uniforms the minute they can. Slaves couldn't doff anything. Just as many private schools specified 'uniforms' for their students so they all tend to look alike (and identify as students of that particular school), so owners of slaves specified their clothing so their possessions would identify as a part of his 'herd' of slaves. [The Roman Senate, fearing that a few slaves were getting too 'uppity' for their status, once passed legislation requiring slaves to wear specific clothing unique to the slave population, but it was quickly repealed when they realized a near majority of Rome's population would now be clearly identified as slaves and it would probably frighten the free population knowing they were almost outnumbered by those presumably under their control.]

Clothing does have a great deal to do with our personal identity - ask any U.S. Marine, a physician with his white coat, a Catholic priest in his clerical garb, a college professor in his academic gown during a commencement exercise, a gang member displaying a particular underwear by his low-riding britches, or a high school athlete flaunting his letter-jacket! Similarly, slaves were frequently forced to display their low status by clothing unique to an owned class.

Social control of slaves was probably even more powerful than physical and psychological devices. Orlando Patterson, a well-known scholar of slavery, claims slaves typically experienced 'social death' by which he means many slaves lost all social identity with their enslavement: their family (including their parents, their marriage partner, their children), their community and/or tribe, often their religious institutions, their name(s), and often even their language. He points out slaves were often transported hundreds (even thousands) of miles away to a new location where the religion was alien, the language was incomprehensible, their social support systems were no longer available, and even their name was changed. Often this was done deliberately to effect dramatic change in a slave's behavior, i.e., it was obvious slaves under these new circumstances did most anything required to survive without rebellion at the price of becoming temporarily despondent and often suicidal. Better despondent than rebellious (suicide could be physically prevented) and the experience of 'social death' made people much more acquiescent to the demands of slavery than any other technique, including extreme beating, starvation, and other drastic measures to assure conformity. Imagine adjusting to a new life where you knew no one, no one spoke your language nor could you understand theirs, no one practiced your religion, you had a whole new name assigned you by others, no one was familiar with the culture you came from, you had no family to call upon for help or support, you had lost your children, wife, or husband forever, and you knew you had no way to ever 'go home' again. What would you do? If you try to kill yourself, it won't be allowed in that you are constantly watched. If you try to starve yourself to death, you will be force-fed. If you are like millions and millions of others, you will eventually adjust to your new circumstances and live your life the best you can with your pre-slavery past becoming more and more a distant memory. I have just described the plight of well over a hundred million slaves over at least 2500 years, including the over 10 million black slaves imported into the Americas over a 400 year period.

Once a slave was sold into a new location (usually with an owner who spoke in an alien language), the slave continued to be controlled by his new society. Social controls included: an owner's mark on his or her body, distinctive clothing, perhaps a collar around her or his neck or an ear-tag permanently attached to tell everyone else you are an owned possession, a name that often denoted slave status, the constant reference to yourself as a 'boy' or 'girl' despite your age, and the reference to you as a 'buck' or 'stud' if male or a 'wench' or 'brood' if female as if you were no different than a horse. In addition legal codes reinforced these social controls in that they often prohibited you from learning anything not allowed by your owner or the state, they prescribed where and where not you could go, they forced you to display respect to free people at every opportunity no matter how repulsive their actions toward you, and they even denied you any rights to your own offspring or the sexual use of your own body. You can get a hint of these types of controls by visiting most any government prison, our closest approximation of the conditions imposed on many slaves historically. Contemporary inmates are only allowed to wear distinctive clothing marking their status, their name is replaced with an assigned number to which they must respond; they are often called 'boy', they are restricted as to where they sleep, who they sleep with, when they can bath, when they can exercise, when they eat (and what they eat), what material they can read, what TV shows they can watch, they must always show respect to their keepers no matter what, they are expected to obey orders instantly and without question, and on and on. One astute long-term jail keeper shared this observation based on his many years of supervising prisoners: "The more controls and restrictions on a prisoner, the more child-like they become to the point where they are mostly concerned with just their basic needs." This observation correlates with many slave owners' comments over the centuries: that their slaves acted like children most of the time and consequently had to be treated as children.

Most slave holding societies rigorously practiced all three types of control: physical, psychological and social. Prevailing religions in slave holding societies tended to strongly reinforce all of these controls as God-given and appropriate as is expounded in the separate chapter on slavery and religion. Is it any wonder that a significant proportion of the earth's population served out their lives as obedient slaves subject to their master's will? This is not to suggest that the slaves enjoyed their slavery or that they didn't long for freedom although a few undoubtedly reached that state of subjugation. But most historical evidence seems to suggest that when given the rare chance of freedom from their masters, slaves almost invariably choose freedom despite the many risks and hardships that such a choice might have led to. The American black slave, where we have the greatest amount of written and oral evidence, strongly supports this conclusion and we can probably safely conclude that most slaves preceding them shared similar aspirations.

Some slaves managed to escape slavery through legitimate means. In Lew Wallace's novel *Ben Hur* the Jewish galley slave Ben Hur rescues a prominent wealthy Roman during a ship wreck and is not only granted his freedom but becomes an adopted son of the Roman noble. In the Old Testament Jacob is sold into slavery by his own brothers and transported to faraway Egypt by the slave dealers who bought him. Years later through hard work, diligence to available opportunities and a lot of good luck, he ends up freed from slavery and a high official in the Egyptian government. The list of such former slaves ending up in prominent positions can be listed by the hundreds.

Other slaves gained freedom illegitimately. Some American black slaves escaped slavery by stealthily running away to Canada via the 'Underground Railway' where they gained free status. Roman runaway slaves were so common the law specified they be branded on the face with a huge "F" (for *fugitivus* in Latin) when caught so that they could be carefully caged and shackled from then on. But undoubtedly many were never caught and managed to live out their lives as 'free' persons.

But whatever their hidden motives, most slaves never gained 'free' status and lived out their lives trying to make themselves as comfortable as possible under the circumstances allowed them. The vast majority of slaves saw the consequences of trying to escape slavery not worth the risks and eventually settled down to where physical restraints weren't needed, they didn't need to be caged or restrained at night, and they didn't need distinctive clothing or collars to remind them of their status. The psychological and social controls in and of themselves worked effectively in their cases. Indeed, many slaves held trusted positions within their owner's household including handling their master's money, tending to their master's health, and educating their master's children. Romans especially extended slaves many liberties which utilized the skills they had obtained prior to being enslaved. Most physicians, teachers and accountants in Roman times were slaves and were generally well treated, even respected for their unique skills if market prices are any indication. [Next time you see your doctor or have an appointment with a professor or your tax specialist, think of him as someone's slave and you'll gain a different perspective!]

Although civil libertarians sometimes claim that all people lust for freedom, history proves that although they may lust for freedom, few slaves took steps to actually obtain freedom, probably because they saw the goal as well nigh impossible within their circumstances. That's what made an effective slave society!

THE ECONOMICS OF SLAVERY

E conomists have long debated whether buying slaves to perform tasks was cheaper than just hiring free labor as needed.

Obviously, investment in slaves requires considerable capital investment or interest on that capital if borrowed, and upkeep (food, shelter, clothing, and health care) of the slaves purchased. Added to that would be depreciation as the slave ages and productivity decreases as well as the risk of a slave's disability, death, theft, or escape.

Hiring free labor would entail none of these costs other than the wages demanded in that the employee would generally be responsible for his own housing, food, clothing and health care. Furthermore, hired help could be terminated once there was no longer a need for his or her services. Slaves would have to be sold at prevailing prices once they were no longer needed.

On the surface it would seem hiring free labor would be considerably simpler, if not cheaper. But slaves, if cheap enough, had advantages too. First, slaves could be assigned to any task, no matter how onerous. Free employees could balk at certain assignments and refuse to do them. Second, slaves could be worked much longer and harder than most free persons would tolerate, no matter what the wages paid, and slaves generally had no recourse from almost endless work and, if necessary, under a whip to insure maximum output. Third, slaves could not leave their work assignments, whereas free hires could quit at any time. This was especially important when necessary job skills had to be learned over a long period. Fourth, slaves could not object to the assignment of new tasks whereas free hires might balk at new demands made upon them.

Fifth, slaves often reproduced themselves, yielding their owners new slaves to add to their profits. Sixth, slaves could be sent to any locale or be hired out to others as needed, whereas free persons generally balked at such transfers without extra considerations.

The disadvantage of slave labor was clearly the initial costs involved as well as the necessity to keep them productive at all times. Hence, if slaves became too costly due to short supply, slave labor at some point became economically unfeasible. Their owners could never recoup their initial investment through the slave's probable work life, let alone pay the interest cost for mortgaged slaves. But where slaves were plentiful, prices were low enough to where a slave could easily repay his cost by only a few years of productive output. [This explains the strong interest in slaves reproducing themselves in that this source of slaves costs very little]. If slaves could not be utilized in productive labor year-round, the cost of slave labor vs. free hires deceased significantly. Consequently, slavery worked best when the slaves themselves could be kept in productive work continually such as multi-crop plantations with long growing seasons, factories, mines, and domestic service. Hired labor proved more economical when the work was seasonal, a single project, or temporary.

A contemporary comparison might be an employer's decision whether to hire a full-time employee or simply contract with a labor provider such as many 'temp help' companies. A modern full time employee carries the burden of health insurance, some form of pension contribution, vacation and sick leave, and severance pay upon termination. Day labor has none of these complications, but brings with it an employee's unfamiliarity with the expected tasks, a possible lack of commitment, and the unknown qualities of who you're hiring.

The most famous (and controversial) study of the costs of slave vs. free labor was done by two economists, Robert Fogel and Stanley Engerman. Their research was reported in a two-volume book entitled *Time on the Cross* (1974). In the book Fogel and Engerman argue that the system of slavery was profitable for U.S. Southern slave owners because they organized plantation production 'rationally' to maximize their profits. Due to economies of scale (the so called 'gang system' of labor on cotton plantations), they purported Southern slave farms were more productive (per unit of labor) than northern U.S. farms. The implication of this Engerman and Fogel contended, is that slavery in the American South was not going away on its own (as it had in some historical instances such as Ancient Rome) because, despite its exploitative nature, slavery was immensely profitable and productive for slave owners. This contradicted the argument of earlier Southern historians.

A portion of *Time on the Cross* focused on how slave owners treated their slaves. Engerman and Fogel argued that because slave owners approached slave production as a business enterprise there were some limits on the amount of exploitation and oppression they inflicted on the slaves. According to Engerman and Fogel, slaves in the American South lived better than did many industrial workers in the North. Fogel based this analysis largely on plantation records and claimed that slaves worked less, were better fed and whipped only occasionally—although the authors were careful to state explicitly that slaves were still exploited in many ways which were not captured by measures available from records. This portion of *Time on the Cross* created a fire-storm of controversy, although it was not directly related to the central argument of the book - that Southern slave plantations were profitable for the slave owners and would not have disappeared in the absence of the Civil War. Some criticisms mistakenly considered Fogel an apologist for slavery. In fact, Fogel objected to slavery on moral grounds; he thought that on purely economic grounds slavery was not unprofitable or inefficient as previous historians had argued.

Many historians promptly rejected several of Fogel and Engerman's conclusions for a variety of technical reasons. Arguments were made that the wrong measurements were used, e.g., determining the harshness of slavery by estimating the number of slaves whipped rather than how often each slave was whipped. Other criticisms were leveled at Fogel and Engerman's lack of including slave motivations such as systematic and regular rewards for work well done and a failure to consider the psychological effect public whipping would have on other slaves. Many critics point out the records studied were from an area where single-crop plantations were concentrated and where slaves had long periods of relative inactivity between crops.

A scattering of subsequent studies done primarily by economists tend to support Fogel and Engerman's main points, adding that rural slaves typically grew most of their own food supply, clothing costs were restricted to yearly issuance of a pair of cheap cotton pants, a shirt or so, a rope belt, and little else, including shoes, and slaves usually even built their own shelter with lumber on hand. Even factory and mining slaves maintenance costs were kept surprisingly low: the cheapest food was the order of the day (often food non-slaves refused to eat such as pig knuckles, hog jowls, and greens); clothing issued was old and minimum; and housing was usually in dorms constructed at little cost. These latter types of slaves were also unaffected by seasonal influences on their work.

Agreeing with the majority of economists, the majority of historians conclude that slavery was usually a very profitable business enterprise. Free labor typically could not compete with slave labor and often led to massive unemployment among the non-slave population. Rome's non-slaves found themselves unable to compete with slaves and formed a huge pool of chronically unemployed living off the public dole. Likewise, Caribbean sugar plantations produced massive wealth when manned by slaves but quickly became economically unfeasible when slavery ended. Historians also note the hidden benefits of slavery within a society: people formerly held in prisons at public expense are simply sold on the auction block thereby bringing in considerable money to the state; the problem of orphans and family abandonment was solved by simply enslaving those problematic persons; and where indebtedness was grounds for enslavement, those owed money got it back through the purchase price of the debtor. Historians also emphasize that many social problems were solved by simply enslaving the problems and ridding society of any responsibility for their welfare (e.g., Britain's shipping its civil problems off as virtual slaves to Australia) and that some governments profited greatly from the proceeds of slave sales. Not lost to historians was that one of the bonuses of owning slaves was 'harvesting' their offspring for added profit.

Marxists and capitalists both forcefully argued that free labor was always cheaper than slave labor in the final analysis because a slave has nothing to gain from working hard for the betterment of his owner's wealth, but this position argues against many thousands of years of widespread slavery in the world. Why would it have maintained itself as long as it did if free labor was in fact more economical? Surely slavery wasn't maintained solely out of historical habit, social custom, the human desire to exert power over others, or even to maintain owner's personal pride and ego. One must remember that slavery was ended because a newly emerged moral sense that owning another human was somehow wrong, not because it wasn't economical.

RACE-RELATED SLAVERY

A t one time, Romans took a fancy to the relatively rare black-skinned slave and paid astronomical prices to own a fine specimen for themselves usually placing them in positions where they would enhance their owner's status by publicly pronouncing her or his wealth. But race-related slavery was almost unique to the New World where African blacks were imported by the millions to meet the labor needs of primarily plantation economies. Although at first, both whites and blacks were being sold in the Americas (primarily in the fledgling European colonies of the Caribbean and North America) as chattel slaves, soon 'indentured servitude' status was afforded whites while blacks remained as 'slaves for life'. By the 17th century, slaves in the Americas were almost entirely black and soon blackness equated with slavery.

But this created many new problems concerning slave status. Manumitted blacks were a special problem and usually had to carry papers with them at all times proving their free status. Freed blacks often found themselves kidnaped, transported to a new location where they were not known and resold as slaves. Since white masters sometimes cohabited with their black female slaves, offspring were of mixed race and their status caused special legal problems that had to be addressed. Generally, any issue of a slave's womb was considered a slave, but some of the babies were white or near white in appearance. Terms such as 'quadroon' (one-fourth black), mulatto (one-half black, the word derived from the Spanish word for mule denoting hybrid status), 'octoroon' (one-eighth black), etc., were all legally classified as slaves by birth, but 'mustees' (those appearing near white often with blond hair and blue eyes) remained a problem in that they could possibly pass as 'free whites' unless measures were taken. Consequently, led by Mississippi, most slave-holding states in the U.S. as well as Brazil set up registries of 'blood origins' of its citizens so that, legally, even 1/32th of black blood in a newborn classified that child as 'colored' and subject, if not the slavery of the 19th century, certainly to the segregationist 'Jim Crow' laws of most southern states which were prevalent until the late 1960s. (Mississippi only closed its blood registry office in the late 1980s in that by that time blood lines were getting hard to follow).

The psychological result of race-related slavery was profound in societies that practiced it. The Antebellum U.S. South, especially, turned racism into a fine art. All slaves were black. The common belief was that blacks were basically animals, inherently inferior, and needed guidance from their superiors. As animals, blacks best responded to treatment like an animal. Physical, social, and psychological coercion, fear, and constraints were all necessary just as they were for effective management of other livestock such as a mule or donkey. Failure to freely employ these techniques allowed their true slavish nature to emerge and predictable problems such as unrestrained licentiousness, inherent sloth and laziness, and moral depravity inevitably resulted. Slavery, where their lives were controlled by their betters, was thought to actually be a blessing for their own best welfare as well as uplifting in their development.

A slave who wasn't black had to be 'made' black one way or another to justify his or her slave status. The way to do this was label him a 'mustee' which meant, a white black. This would suggest the white had some black in him somehow and therefore justified him or her being held as a slave. A careful search of the slave's physique and physiology usually managed to reveal presumably hidden traces of Negro blood in them. These traits were usually hints of features typical of many blacks such as kinky hair, thick lips, wide flat noses, and 'yellowed' eyes. Blacks were also thought to have bigger builds and larger muscular structure than whites which revealed their draft animal status. Similarly, blacks were thought to be simple-minded, even childlike, in their mental abilities, not unlike most other domestic animals. Blacks' sexual organs were also thought to be relatively large, more comparative to animals such as horses than humans (whites), reflective of their animalistic sexual lust which generally had to be controlled one way or another.

A white possessing any of these features could easily be accused of being a black in disguise and therefore most whites were very careful to flaunt their exclusive white traits at every opportunity and hide those traits that might be associated with blackness. White women avoided the sun at all costs to avoid risking any skin darkening possibilities and face powders and other makeup were always as white as possible. Light colored hair and blue or green eyes, highly unusual among blacks, was seen as the ideal standard and much admired. Among white men excessive muscular development was avoided, clothing was highly stylized away from practicality, and performing manual labor of any type was left to those 'born to it'. Wit, verbosity, and a commanding tone in the voice were highly valued traits in that they clearly distinguished the master race from the slave race.

Black behavior was rigidly specified to meet these social expectations. Therefore, small, non-muscular blacks were devalued as 'runts' or 'defects'; blacks who were articulate or verbose were viewed as 'uppity' and 'smart-mouthed' and subject to severe but necessary 'correction'. Blacks dressed up in white's clothing were seen condescendingly as amusing 'dandified pets' or 'showpieces' of their masters rather than the practical work animals that resided beneath that fancy clothing. Black males were expected to be 'randy' and needed heavy supervision to subvert a constant threat to the sanctity of white women while black females were thought to be so wanton and morally depraved that they enjoyed engaging in sex with anybody at any opportunity. These latter traits led to blacks being perceived as exceptionally good sexual playmates, rapacious in their reproduction, but dangerous in their licentiousness.

Racism was so embedded, so developed, so perfected in the Southern United States of that time that it affected the victimized blacks themselves as well as the white masters. Blacks raised in such an environment actually thought that the lighter the skin, the better the person; that whites were smarter and brighter than blacks as a rule; that blacks were probably much better at manual labor than whites and therefore were probably born to do that; and that blacks enjoyed sex more because they had greater interest in it and did it better than their white masters. Believing some of this, blacks often risked imitating whites in speech, clothing, behavior and even looks. Hair straightening, hair bleaching, highly stylized clothing, and exaggerated articulated speech patterns became almost comical in their imitative efforts and soon became the butt of white's jokes and characterizations which quickly embedded themselves in the rubric of stereotypes.

And whites got trapped in the same environment. Manual labor became despised along with poor 'white trash' that still had to perform the tasks slaves normally did. Exclusive white characteristics such as blue eyes, light-colored hair, etc., became idealized along with white society's own cherished concepts of exclusive moral righteousness. White religions began to support and uphold white superiority as God-given and divinely inspired.

The legal system, controlled entirely by whites, encapsulated all of these beliefs into a legal code which was designed to keep things just like they were and ward off any potential threats to the status quo.

Unfortunately these racist concepts were so ingrained in the society that, even over 140 years following the end of black slavery in the Americas (Brazil didn't abolish slavery until 1877), some of these ideas still linger here and there and are the source of many social problems within these former slaveholding societies.

RELIGION AND SLAVERY

The argument has been made that Christian peoples at least tended not to enslave those like themselves. In England where approximately one in ten were slaves at the time the Doomsday book was published around 1000 A.D., slaves were being changed to serfs relatively early in European history.

But by the 18th century the British nevertheless managed to send large numbers of their society's unwanted off as virtual slaves (sometimes labeled 'indentured servants' or 'transports') to colonies that needed cheap labor. Many of these English (and later Irish and Scot) citizens were disenfranchised due to debt, petty crimes, and chronic unemployment and were massively run through English courts to receive sentences of indenture ranging from five years to lifetime. Once sentenced, they were shipped off to English colonies throughout the world (the Caribbean possessions, the United States colonies [particularly Georgia], Australian penal colonies in Sydney and later Perth, and coal mines in Scotland). These 'slaves' (certainly lifetime indenture constitutes slavery) were sold at auction the same as any other commodity, had no civil status or rights, and were usually treated little better than livestock. But once they had been English citizens! They were predominately white and either Anglican or Catholic in religious faith. This enslavement of its own people was at no time condemned by the Church or England or the Catholic Church in Ireland. For years history books either overlooked this mass enslavement of whites or made it appear such slaves were mainly house servants or apprentices of a trade and that most were limited in their servitude to a relatively short length of time - just enough to pay for their passage to the New World.

Newer scholarship points out most 'indentured servants' were 'servants for life', were usually bought for tasks involving huge expenditures of energy, and were often worked to death especially in the Caribbean plantations where they often worked side by side next to African slaves in the sugar cane fields where an overseer's whip was thought necessary to extract a slave's maximum potential. The next time you look at a chain gang of sentenced prisoners mowing the grass or picking up trash alongside a major highway, usually with little to no pay for their labor and with no options to do anything other than what the state has proscribed for them, you may be gently reminded of those 'indentured servants' of long ago.

Slavery is often thought of conceptually as the opposite of freedom. But freedom is much harder to define than slavery and most religions toy around with the term 'freedom.' Are you 'free' through Christ, as Christianity often proclaims? Was a slave physically bonded to his earthly owner but spiritually free through his or her belief in a Redeeming Savior? The Apostle Paul repeatedly told slaves of his time that very message. Recent archeological excavations of Corinth (Greece), where Paul lived a good part of his life, have identified where Paul lived and where he often preached. The path between the two places takes you right by Corinth's huge slave market so it is likely Paul passed this market many a time in his daily life. Yet in all his letter writing he never once condemns slavery per se or the selling of fellow human beings or the plight of a slave owned by a cruel master despite undoubtedly seeing the reality of slavery as an everyday occurrence. This is not to condemn the Apostle Paul but simply to point out that what is common to us is seldom seen as wrong and Paul was as much a product of his culture as any other man.

Consequently it is easy to see how many ministers and religious leaders justified slavery over the years - they grew up with it, were surrounded by people of like mind about the institution of slavery, and could justify it by the Holy Book. Specifically, the New Testament preaches for slaves to accept their fate, obey their earthly master no matter what and dwell upon a presumably better (although very vague) afterlife where anguish and worry are no more.

The word 'Islam' literally means submission. Submission to God, true. But spiritual and even bodily submission to someone beyond yourself is inherent in the religion. Hence its emphasis on fasting, the discipline of scheduled prayer (which involves a physical act of obeisance), and the belief that God rules all aspects of your life. For example, if enslaved, it must be part of God's plan or you wouldn't find yourself in that predicament.

Western slave traders were always amazed at Islamic practitioners' 'acceptance' of their enslavement. This doesn't mean they liked what had happened to them or that they didn't resist their captors, but that they accommodated to their new status eventually as perhaps one aspect of 'fate' interpreted as 'in the hands of God.'

It is not surprising then that Muslims never directly questioned slavery itself (this could easily be interpreted as part of 'God's will') but did make efforts to make it a kinder, more gentle form of slavery than most Christian plantation owners did. Manumission of a devoted and loyal slave was seen as an act bringing honor and respect to the manumitter, care of an aged or sick slave was seen as a moral duty, and many slaves were treated as a member of the family with definite obligations to serve his master/mistress but with many of the privileges of a family member such as protection, some security, adequate diet, decent clothing, and a feeling of belonging to a recognized social unit. "I am the slave of _____ " as a self-description gave a slave an identity, a family unit to lock onto, and security similar to an offspring saying "My father is _____" as a way of identifying him or herself within society. This certainly was a different form of slavery than a nameless chained slave on a Roman latifundium (plantation) who was treated no different from a horse and cost one-fifth as much or a plantation slave in Jamaica where the only non-slave you ever saw was the overseer whose relationship with you was that he had the whip in his hand at all times and you received the whip on your back the minute you slowed down.

Muslims are enjoined not to newly enslave those of the faith, although those born into it or who are already slaves remain in that station. Hence Arab slavers typically sought out new slaves in non-Muslim territories (mainly 'pagan' Africa and Christian Russia) for sale throughout the Middle East and Northern Africa. But this injunction was widely ignored when convenient and Muslims enslaved Muslims, especially if

43

huge profits were involved. Muslims were imperious in enslaving 'pagan' African blacks by the millions; they had few qualms about emasculating a considerable number of male slaves into eunuchs for one purpose or another; and seemed to have a penchant for placing slaves into humiliating positions through distinctive costume, superfluous duties, or flaunting them as a symbol of their wealth.

The fact slavery is treated so casually in the Koran as part of society's fabric and the fact slaves were generally treated as fellow human beings, not human livestock, is perhaps the reason legal slavery endured in the Arab world longer than any other place on earth. While black slaves were being freed in the New World on a massive scale in the 19th century, slavery flourished in the Arab world and Muslim areas of Asia until the mid to late 20th century, when it too finally ended.

Jews never condemned slavery and practiced it almost universally with a few exceptions here and there. This is particularly surprising in the fact that Jews themselves were often the enslaved, rather than the slavers. Although some scholars now question whether Jews were actually enslaved in Egypt (but merely lived as aliens there), there is no question Jews were mainly slaves in ancient Babylon, certainly at the time of Alexander the Great, in huge numbers during the time of the Roman Empire, later throughout Europe during the first 14 centuries and as recently as the mid-20th century by the Germans. Nevertheless, Jews who owned slaves were enjoined to treat slaves as fellow humans (not bought livestock), to give them adequate rest and nutrition, and to at least consider manumission of slaves who had served them for many years with loyalty and devotion.

Hinduism doesn't have much to say about slavery one way or the other although it was widely practiced in areas where Hinduism was the major faith. Perhaps this is because the 'caste' system already made huge distinctions among peoples in society, placing the 'untouchables' in a social position similar to slaves in other cultures. The 'untouchable' caste may have derived from people in chattel slavery originally in that they were relegated to work which others found beneath their dignity, were prohibited from marrying upwards in society, their children were automatically restricted to the untouchable caste with no way out of it, and most social advantages, e.g., education, prestige, and earning opportunities, were denied them by nature of their birth. The fact that most 'untouchables' were very dark-skinned relative to those above them in social status easily identified them within their society. Just recently an 'untouchable' was attempting to enter a university in India through the courts, but to date his admission was still being denied. 'Untouchables' captured and sold off in other lands (primarily in Africa and the Persian Gulf) as slaves had little difficulty adjusting to their new circumstances which added to their market value. This is probably because they noticed little difference in their life circumstances - being an 'untouchable' in India was so similar to chattel slavery in the Persian Gulf it is doubtful the only difference they observed was that now other people were actually buying and selling them.

Hinduism places great emphasis on acceptance of the social status you are born into and practically no emphasis on trying to change your position in society. Since this life is temporary, you hope for a better life in your reincarnation where indeed you might be born into vastly different circumstances (including a non-human form). Indians, especially of the lower castes, proved easy to obtain on the subcontinent, were quick to adjust to being actual slaves, and saw little need to object or rebel to their slavery in that their lives now were just a brief journey anyway and fate was not to be questioned. These traits are exactly what made them premium choices at Middle Eastern and African slave markets.

Other eastern religions (e.g., Buddhism, Sikhism, Zoroastrianism, Taoism, Confucianism, Shintoism, etc.) do not really mention slavery as an institution although it was widely practiced throughout the Eastern countries. In fact there is no country in the Far East that didn't practice widespread slavery for many centuries, so at any given time millions of people served as slaves to their owners in all Asian and Middle Eastern countries. Most Far Eastern religions put heavy emphasis on acceptance of one's life. If you end up a slave (or are born into it), then it is 'godly' to accept that fate and live righteously within whatever social position the gods have placed you. The most notable exception is Genghis Khan, who was born into slavery but was freed and later ruled a goodly percentage of the world's population. But even having an ex-slave as an international leader didn't alter the institution of slavery - the Mongol Empire practiced slavery on a wide scale and Mongol slaves were treated no better than slaves anywhere else in the world.

THE HUMAN FASCINATION
WITH POWER OVER OTHERS

I n the 1960s Stanley Milgram, a social psychologist, revealed a study
he had completed which attempted to measure how far people
will go in obeying authority. He undertook the study in part for
personal reasons: both his parents had been exterminated in 'death
camps' by ordinary German SS soldiers who managed to efficiently
and methodically murder over 6 million people during a three year
period during World War II. Milgram realized that the first people
murdered had been chronic social problems (severely mentally retarded,
physically handicapped, or mentally ill) and had been 'euthanized' with
little protest and considerable praise from the German populace during
late 1930s. When the program was expanded to other social 'deviants'
(homosexuals, Gypsies, Communists and other political protesters),
protest movements arose but were relatively insignificant. Still later, the
program was expanded to include a minority religious group, Jews, who
made up a significant portion of Germany's (and their conquered areas)
populace. This last expansion was officially kept secret, but hundreds
of thousands of people were in on the secret, especially the SS elite
soldier corps who actually carried out the killings, numerous contractors
building and maintaining 'death' camps and civilian hires who did most
of the supervisory work.

Even though six million people were killed in this German program
of racial purification (now labeled the 'Holocaust'), many more than that
number were used as slave laborers first along with millions of others

(mainly prisoners of war, conquered peoples, political opponents, etc.) who were simply enslaved for the cheap, controllable labor they provided for the German economy. Overall, counting the Jews, homosexuals, Gypsies, etc., who were worked as slaves prior to their scheduled extermination, it is estimated the Germans had over 10 million people working as unpaid laborers for them during the early 1940s who were housed, clothed, fed and disciplined no different than slaves since time immemorial. This episode of slavery was continued in the 1950s in the Stalinist era of the former U.S.S.R (in the areas now called Russia, Belorussia, and the Ukraine) where an estimated four million German prisoners, political protesters, those peoples resisting Soviet occupation (in Poland, Hungary, Romania, Serbia, and Bulgaria primarily) were shipped to 'gulags' (work camps) in Siberia as literal slaves. This brief period (1938-1965) was the last great episode of a legalized, government-sponsored, and very institutionalized form of slavery.

Dr. Milgram, like many others, realized that enslaving (and methodically killing) millions of people took a lot of people obeying orders to make it work. Why would ordinary people obey orders to enslave (and kill) millions of their fellow citizens who basically looked like them, were educated like them and who they had lived with for many generations? He designed a rather simple experiment with ordinary American college students where they were asked by a white-coated college professor/researcher to coach presumably other fellow students into quickly learning a rather simple word-association task. The students were told the administration of mild electric shocks for learning errors quickened the learning process - they were asked to administer the electric shocks when the learners made errors - the shocks increasing in intensity with the frequency of learning errors. The 'learners', actually professional actors imitating reactions to shock where they couldn't be seen by the student coaches, verbally protested as the shocks increased in intensity, finally screaming in agony as the shocks presumably became extremely painful. When the student coaches protested at hurting others, they were told coldly but officiously by the white-coated 'doctor' that they had to continue in order for the experiment to be completed. Milgram found that very few of the student coaches actually refused to carry the 'torture' through to completion; all the others obeyed the authority figure in completing their task although many were glad when their role in the experiment was over. When asked if they had qualms about their role, most replied that the learner should have learned faster, no real harm would come of it in that it was 'university approved', or that they must have been assigned a particularly uncooperative learner who wasn't paying attention to the task at hand and that he 'deserved' to be punished. Milgram concluded that even innocent American undergraduates were little different in obeying orders regardless of what they were asked to do than the Nazi SS soldiers two decades earlier. Both groups were about the same age, both had received about the same amount of education, and both were raised in relatively stable households. Milgram's radical experiment investigating human social behavior was shocking at the time, is still shocking today and has never been replicated in that it could have psychologically damaged the participants, a fact Milgram himself acknowledged later. Milgram used only male subjects in his experiment because the Nazi soldiers obeying their superiors were all male so what women would do in a similar experimental setting is not known to this day.

A decade later Dr. Phillip Zimbardo, a social psychology at Stanford University, conducted another study investigating the effects of social role in exerting power over others and submitting to authority. In this experiment Zimbardo randomly placed volunteer undergraduate students into two groups. The first group of 'prisoners' were arrested in their homes, hand-cuffed and taken to a 'jail' in the basement of the university's psychology department made to look like a detention facility, stripped, given only a brief tunic to wear and locked into a cell - all these 'prisoners' knew they were part of a prolonged experiment. The second group were given instructions on how to be a prison 'guard', were dressed in appropriate guard uniforms complete with a baton fastened to a wide belt, a visored hat and mirrored sunglasses. The second group was told their task was to make the 'prisoners' obey the prison rules (rules not dissimilar to rules practiced in most U.S. jails and prisons) which emphasized lining up, counting off, doing chores as commanded, keeping the quarters neat and orderly, and showing proper respect to the guards in charge of them. Within five days the experiment had to be stopped: the 'guards' had become so abusive to their 'prisoners' there was the potential of physical damage; the 'prisoners' were so submissive and depressed there was the potential of psychological damage. Both groups were playing their assigned roles too well.

The 'guards' had become bullies flaunting their authority at every chance, making their charges perform meaningless tasks just to demonstrate their authority over them and were assuming they were superior in most every way to those assigned the 'prisoner' role. Some of the guards, even in five days, were becoming cruel, both psychologically and physically, in their behavior toward their fellow students. The 'prisoners' were playing their assigned role so well they thought they were deserving of their treatment, thought they had no right to protest unjust or unreasonable commands, and were meek and servile in both behavior and attitude.

Zimbardo suggested that role assignment is a powerful tool and explained abuses of power so common in prisons and jails throughout the world. Now, 50 years later, we read almost daily of serious physical, psychological and sexual abuses toward those incarcerated globally.

In 2004, for example, The Baghdad Correctional Facility (commonly called Abu Ghraib Prison) was exposed as a nest of human abuse, this time by both enlisted men and officers of the United States Army occupying Iraq. When the TV show "*60 Minutes*" and the *New Yorker Magazine* broke the story with accompanying photos leaked out of the prison, Americans and Iraqi both saw instances of U.S. servicemen performing physical, psychological, and sexual abuse on Iraqi prisoners under their jurisdiction. Photos of unbelievable physical tortures, rape, sodomy, enforced nakedness, prisoners forced to perform sex with fellow prisoners in public, prisoners being led around by leashes attached to dog collars, prisoners being forced to masturbate for their guard's entertainment, prisoners being forced to denounce their God, etc., shocked Americans and enraged Iraqis. Even worse photographs were suppressed by the United States government on the grounds it might 'worsen Iraqi-U.S. relations' - perhaps the greatest understatement of all times.

What's the point of reviewing all this? Simply to demonstrate that modern man, despite his (relative) high level of education, his civilization, his developed religious thought, his sense of human decency, etc., can be just as calloused toward the welfare of his fellow human beings as the cruelest taskmaster whipping the Jewish slaves in Ancient Rome building the Coliseum, as insensitive to the suffering of others as the overseers of black slaves in the gold mines of Peru who whipped slaves to death within six months of entering their new work environment, or the SS Colonel Eichmann who planned the systematic gassing and cremation of millions of Jews simply because they were 'non-Aryan.' Perhaps Milgram's and Zimbardo's experiments reveal a truth about ourselves we'd rather forget, i.e., that domination over others is addictive and that, given the opportunity, that quality of exercising power over others rises to the surface. (Sigmund Freud in his writing of the 1920s suggested that one of society's main functions was to keep human's sadomasochistic tendencies under control.)

The history of slavery certainly suggests that! Ordinary people take on the role of 'master' with little difficulty and ordinary people act like 'slaves' simply because the role is prescribed rather definitely for them by society. The allure of dominating others (or of being dominated by others) certainly helps explain why millions took on the role of literally owning another human being(s), 'breaking' that human to his will, and then desensitizing him to the plight of simply being an owned object, no different than other property. Prescribed roles also helps explain why so little rebellion was observed in slave societies where a sizeable percentage of the population were treated little different than other owned animals and where the demanded tasks of these 'properties' were frequently undesirable, unceasing, and monotonous.

At this point it is interesting to ask yourself two questions. If you were born into a society where slavery was well-established and suddenly were enslaved, exactly how would you adjust to your new status given the restrictions and boundaries inherent in that society? Likewise, ask yourself, in that same society, if given the means and opportunities to own another person to do what you don't like to do, to please you in any way possible, and which would give you the social prestige and personal sense of power that only owning another person offers, how would you respond?

Possible Personal
Perspectives Of A
Slave Dealer, A Slave
Master, And A Slave

I n an attempt to make the topic of historical slavery more real, I
have added some narratives describing a fictional 15ᵗʰ century slave
dealer in Arabia, a normative slave master in Rome during the early
part of the Empire, and a composite female slave in the Antebellum
South (United States). In each instance, I have tried to encapsulate a
particular perspective which samples various aspects of slavery within a
specific geographical region during a time when bondage of others was a
flourishing enterprise. These stories are just that - stories - but the hope is
to demonstrate to the reader how slavery can be viewed quite differently
depending on whether you are earning your living through trade in other
human beings, through owning other people outright with the intent of
using them to increase your wealth or inflate your ego, or actually being
an owned object where others exercise all rights over you, including your
body which now belongs to someone else.

I picked these three periods of slave history in that all of them
represent major aspects of world slavery. The Roman Empire had more
slaves than any other power up to that time. It not only held millions
in slavery but it reduced slaves to the status of livestock. "Speaking
animals" was the common perspective of the Empire's vast holdings of
these subspecies of humans.

The Arab slave trade prospered from around 700 A.D. all the way through to the 20th century - one of the longest-lived trades in world history. It was more charitable than Roman slavery in general but plundered Africa of much of its population over more than 13 centuries.

The period of slavery most familiar to Americans was also the shortest-lived: less than 400 years in length, slavery in the Southern United States (and much of the Caribbean and South America) was the only slavery based entirely on the subjugation of one race over another, white over black. It, like the Romans, was often cruel and unfeeling but lathered with a coating of Christian benevolence claiming to be ultimately helping those inferior to themselves in all ways except physical strength and endurance.

In all three illustrated periods, though, the motives for human slavery remained the same: it was quite profitable; it handled various social problems; and it provided the manpower necessary to do what others didn't want to do. Slavery in all time periods also allowed the privileged few to enjoy lording it over others - those who had either lost in battle and were enslaved, were born into slavery, or found themselves slaves by kidnaping, parental sale, self-sale, piracy, etc.

FASIL AL-KHALIFA, THE ARAB SLAVE DEALER

Early 15th Century

"Get that new batch into their cages, Tariq," Fasil Al-Khalifa barked at his slave assistant. Fasil Al-Khalifa, a handsome man in his fifties, had been in the slave business for close to three decades now and there wasn't much he didn't know about the trade by this time. His wealth attested to his acuity in the trade. Tariq, on the other hand, was born into slavery but only recently had been acquired by his new master, who was intent on training him on the ins and outs of acquiring and selling slaves for his owner's profit. Tariq was born to an Egyptian slave woman but, judging from his features, had a lot of Greek blood in him. His new master had named him 'Tariq', a good Arab name, rather than the Egyptian name 'Safar' he had before.

"Master, how many did you buy this time?" Tariq asked.

"Just 85 this time, but that African chief had promised me at least a 100. That last village raid wasn't as fruitful as he had hoped and besides they foolishly killed off some that probably would have been marketable. He admitted they killed off some of the children and most of those showing grey hair. These Africans have no concept of what you can get at a decent market for even those they consider not worth the bother of shackling and holding them for me." Fasil spit in disgust at the stupidity of those he had to deal with to get his human commodities.

"Most all black as usual," Tariq mumbled to himself as he dutifully picked up his whip to herd the new goods into the crude building holding the cages and cells his master had carefully constructed years ago to hold his stock until a scheduled auction took place right in front of this very building.

With Tariq's whip whistling over their heads, the shackled slaves shuffled inside the building and in groups of 6, were thrust into the various cages. Later Tarif would enter each cell and unshackle them one by one while one of his master's guards stood outside in case a new slave decided to rebel. Still later he would lead them on-by-one on a leash fastened to their neck collar to the washing area where each slave would be ordered to eliminate his body wastes and then wash his entire body with cold water and a mixture of sand, ash and palm oil prior to being fed a coarse gruel of boiled grain, a little lamb, and honey. By the time all 85 had been cleansed and fed, Tariq and the ever-present guards (slaves themselves) would be exhausted.

When Tariq reported to his master that all the slaves had been cleansed and fed and were safely in their cells, Fasil merely nodded and reminded Tariq that in the morning the new slaves would need to be properly branded, refitted with 'sales' collars, and thoroughly examined to determine how to best present them at the auction for the best price.

The slave guards were used to the branding process and, binding the slaves tightly to a branding table so the hot iron could be applied cleanly, i.e., without the slave wiggling around to make a messy burn. Each slave had to be turned over in that the slave mark of ownership was usually applied both front and back (usually the hip and the chest) for ready identification of the slave's new status. Tariq's job was to keep the branding irons hot in the fire so they were always ready when a slave had been properly strapped down. He hated the smell of flesh burning all day, but the guards barely seemed to notice - probably they had grown used to it. Tariq ignored their screams of anguish - after all he had been branded when he was of age, so he viewed it little differently than being fitted with a collar or being sold. Brandings, along with many other events in a slave's life, were simply accepted as the fate of any slave and weren't taken personally. He did remember, however, that being branded drilled into his consciousness that he was now property and would always be owned by someone or another.

"Quiet, slave," one of the guards yelled at one of the slaves still squalling long after the brand had left his body. "It will heal nicely in a couple of weeks and you won't even notice it."

When the slave still didn't shut up, the other guards took his whip to the slave's back and after a few strokes of the vicious metal-tipped flog the slave simply passed out with blood running down his back.

"There, a least he's quiet now," the guard said with some satisfaction as he dragged the defeated slave back to his cage.

Tariq was used to this as a slave himself and thought little of it. In fact, he too was angry at the stupid slave making such a commotion over an act any slave knew would happen at some point. After all, Tariq thought, slaves need to have some mark of ownership on them and, in Tariq's view, it was better than clipping his ears, putting a ring through his nose, or branding him on his forehead as he'd seen had been done to some slaves owned by a less kind master.

At the end of the second day Tariq had witnessed the branding of the new lot of slaves and supervised their cleansing and feeding for the next two weeks when their burns had healed and the forthcoming auction would be held. His master Fasil checked that he was doing his tasks properly from time to time and when Tariq had noted an infection from one of the brands and had treated it appropriately with some medicinal salve, Fasil rewarded him with an extra food ration that had considerable meat in it as well as a night with one of Fasil's female household slaves their master was hoping to breed. That particular female slave had already produced two healthy babies for her master, each with a different slave father and took to this coupling with a resigned detachment of total disinterest which Tariq ignored since such an opportunity wasn't allowed him very often. But Tariq did ponder what it might be like to be able to pick a woman of your own, actually know the woman over a period of time in a meaningful relationship, and be able to know your own children. Only free people could indulge themselves in such luxuries he concluded.

"Tariq," Fasil said rather sharply, "tomorrow is the auction as you well know. Are all the slaves ready to be inspected?"

"Yes, master," Tariq answered contritely with his eyes lowered. "They will be cleansed especially well in the early morning and coated with palm oil until they gleam, master. We will shackle their wrists to their neck collars so their body is fully exposed for a buyer's inspection. Master, do you want them covered with a loin cloth, a tunic, or totally exposed at this auction?"

"A loin cloth should do fine. They're easy enough to discard if a buyer is interested in seeing all that he might be buying. But slaves always hold up to the inspections a little better if we give them a little dignity," Fasil chuckled. "They can always check out the goods whether they have a covering or not."

"Yes, master," Tariq replied with a smile on his face. "We've got a nice supply of clean white cotton ones available." Tariq remembered where he was presented totally uncovered at the auction where Fasil bought him and where his public nudity only added to the misery of being sold.

"Tariq, I want you to pay close attention to when I go to the holding cells and tentatively price out each slave - at least set the minimum bid we will accept. You need to learn how to do this accurately and the only way is to learn through experience. You write on this tablet the slave's number and the minimum bid for each slave after I examine each one."

With that Fasil strode off to the holding cells with Tariq following him, wax tablet and stylus in hand. Fasil examined each slave in his cell where he had been kept nude since the day he arrived. He checked their eyes, their hair, their teeth, the body structure, and their musculature, explaining to Tariq what he was doing and why as he went along. Finally, he announced a minimum bid price for the slave, again carefully explaining to Tariq how he arrived at the price, taking into account current market prices, what buyers were looking for currently, and a slave's particular strong sales appeal. He also told Tariq what type of buyer he thought would be interested in that slave and for what purpose.

Tariq paid close attention to his master throughout the entire day, carefully noting the minimal bids for each slave and studying the vast knowledge his master demonstrated in assessing the goods he was planning to sell the next day. He knew the more he learned these skills himself, the more valuable he would be to his owner, the less likely he would be sold off and the more likely he would receive special considerations and privileges in the future. He was well aware some slaves were so skilled in what their masters valued that they were more like business associates than mere slaves of their owner.

Faisal revealed to Tariq what he had paid the African chief for the lot of 85 and, quickly adding up the minimum bids for each of the 85, calculated the amount of profit he could expect if even minimum bids were obtained.

"Tarif, I'll probably make a lot more profit than that," Faisal smirked. "If I don't get minimum bids on a given piece of property, I'll simply have you take it back to the pens until the next auction. I seldom have to lower a minimum until they don't sell through at least three auctions. After that, I lower the price in that I can't feed them forever, you know."

"No master," Tarif responded."Let's hope all sell at the auction, master."

"You get them looking their best and make sure they have the right attitude and we'll sell the whole lot of them," Faisal smiled. "Tell them if they don't sell they'll sure as hell wish they had - a whip and some missed meals changes their attitude toward selling themselves off real fast. Remind them of that, Tarif," he advised.

Tarif was quick with numbers and noted his master would get back more than twice what he had paid for the slaves. He also realized it didn't cost much to 'process' and feed the slaves for market even if they were in the cages for several weeks. Most of the help in handling the new goods were slaves themselves. Tarif also knew that slaves usually sold well above the minimum set for their sale in which case his master profited even more. Like many slaves Tarif knew the more prosperous his master, the better off he would be in terms of food, clothing, and shelter. Furthermore, again like most slaves, he took pride in belonging to a rich man - even a man's human property shared in the prestige of a successful master or mistress.

The next morning, the auction of the 85 new slaves was conducted following a three hour period where potential buyers could inspect the goods for sale any way they wanted. This was tiring (as well as utterly humiliating) for the slaves since they were usually chained in place. If they didn't realize they were mere chattel goods by this point, the inspection period, like the branding before, drove the point home - usually for a lifetime.

By the time the auction took place the slaves for sale were practically numb despite the fact that their entire future depended on who bought them and for what purpose. Were they to be a construction slave? A household slave? An agricultural slave? A galley slave? And what was their new owner to be like? A master heavy with the whip? A mistress with wanton motives? A corporation who would give you a number, feed you just enough to keep you alive, and work you to an early grave in order to extract maximum profit on their investment?

Tariq knew exactly what was going through their minds. It was the same as when he had been sold to his current master, Faisal.

"Tariq, we sold off all the bastards and almost all of them at well above their minimum bids," Faisal said with a smile of satisfaction at the end of the auction and all the sold slaves had been led off to their new homes. "You did a good job of preparing them for the auction. They all looked clean and attractive and never once did I see any of them acting up or struggling in their chains. I don't know what you told them about seeking out a good master or mistress, but apparently whatever you told them they took to heart."

"Thank you, master. I simply reminded them every slave not sold at a good price would get the whipping of their life and probably be sold off to the mines," Tariq risked a quick smile at his master.

Taking the risk of talking to his master directly, Tariq added, "You're in a good business, master. You can make a lot of money selling slaves if you are highly skilled and have great knowledge in that area like you have, master."

"I'm glad you noticed, Tariq," Faisal replied. "Pay attention to your master and you'll learn many of those skills yourself, slave." With that, Faisal did something he had never done before. He reached over and ruffled his slave's hair affectionately. "We'll need to get you a better tunic to let everyone know you're my assistant now, Tariq."

CENTURIUS, THE ROMAN SLAVE MASTER

Early 1st Century

C enturius grabbed his slave whip and headed to the stables. His steward, the slave he had named Canis in honor of a dog he was fond of, had just reported one of Centurius' new purchases had talked back to the steward in a churlish manner when ordered to muck out one of the horses' stalls.

"What punishment did you mete out, Canis?" Centurius asked as he and Canis headed to the horse barn.

"Three lashes across the back with the standard slave whip, master," Canis replied, "but he needs further discipline in my opinion, master. This isn't the first incident, master," Canis explained. "Ever since you bought him last spring he's been moody and uncooperative at times. The whip seems to be the only thing he really listens to, master. May I suggest use of the iron-tipped whip, master? It will tear up his back, but he may learn at last what's expected of a Roman slave."

"Where's the bastard from, Canis?" Centurius asked.

"Thrace, I believe, master. I've never had trouble with Thracians before, but, of course, I think he's new to slavery."

"True, Canis. When I bought him he was a fresh captive of our legions in that cursed region. One of the Thracian barbarians who foolishly resisted our civilizing occupation and soon found himself in chains," Centurius smiled. "We'll break him to his new station soon enough."

Soon the errant Thracian slave, now hitched to a post in the barn by a chain linked to his heavy neck collar, saw his owner for the second time in his life - once when he had been sold to this wealthy Roman who owned vast farms, mines, and small factories from Capua all the way to Rome - and now alongside the slave's main overseer.

"You're my property now and you will do what my steward says quickly, to the best of your ability, and certainly with no comments or dark looks. You're a slave now, no different than any of the other animals I have on this farm, and you were bought to yield to your owner everything you body can produce until the day you die. You can die now under the whip or you can live by starting to act like the slave you are destined to be. While you're thinking about it, we'll give you a small sample of the whips we use for serious infractions so you will have the opportunity to learn what being a slave is all about. You Thracian boys buckle under soon enough, but," Centurius chuckled, "you're slow learners and sometimes we have to beat you half to death before that happens."

Two nearby guards, themselves slaves, were called who under the master's commands chained the Thracian slave between two posts so his body was fully exposed. One of those guards with a mere utterance from his master retrieved a whip with 12 strands, each tipped with bits of sharpened iron, and with no preliminaries proceeded to beat the slave until he slumped in his chains fully unconscious from the horrible pain and then proceeded to give him 30 more lashes until his back was fully opened to raw flesh and a mass of blood.

"Pour salt on the bastard's back when he comes around," Centurius instructed his steward, "and put him on half-rations and only one skin of water a day for five days so the lesson can soak in. No rest for the bastard just because his back is cut up - he's to be put to full duties the minute he can stand up. Use the whip heavily to make sure he gives a full day's work. As you know, Canis, I don't believe in coddling the human livestock."

"Of course not, Master," Canis replied, "but it may die if no recovery period is scheduled," he added with little emotion, using 'it' instead of 'he' to indicate the slave was nothing but mere property.

"Let fate take its course, Canis. It would be a good lesson for the other slaves - besides Thracians are cheap enough these days what with the recent conquests."

Centurius smiled inwardly as a distant memory from his childhood presented itself. He was only 10 at the time and his father had ordered a new litter slave, a young German boy around 18 or so, to the whipping post for stumbling while carrying him on a recent journey. The newly enslaved boy thought the punishment ordered was unfair and cursed his master which lead to a lash across his back instantly. The boy reacted by not only spitting on his master but struck Centurius' father in his face - a fatal gesture in that no Roman slave ever dared to strike their master no matter what. When the guards had subdued the agitated slave and fastened him to the whipping post, his father calmly ordered the slave to be whipped to death for his effrontery. All the other slaves were summoned to witness the execution as a lesson in what awaited them if they were harboring similar thoughts questioning their master's jurisdiction over his property.

As the 10-year-old Centurius watched the boy slowly and painfully agonize under the overseer's iron-tipped whip, he not only felt sorry for the young slave but, shamefully, vomited in reaction to the savagery in front of him.

"Centurius, be a man," his father shouted, obviously embarrassed by the weakness of his son. "Rome's greatness if based on the sternness and self-discipline of its citizens. Why else are we masters of the world? Of course, slaves must be disciplined as needed. How else can we expect them to respond to their masters appropriately? A Roman master sometimes finds himself in the position of properly disciplining a slave - why, the boy actually struck me! Of course he has to be put to death. He should thank me for not crucifying him as the law specifies, but you notice never once did he thank me - slaves so ungrateful are best put down with the whip as you just witnessed. Instead of getting sick over it, you should be glad you had a sensible father who follows the principles that have served Rome so well over the centuries: severity, discipline, adherence to the law, and the ability to manage his property effectively and appropriately. Slaves must not only respect their masters, but fear them. For deep within any slave, it is fear that breaks them to our will. Romans understand that and use fear effectively, both in war and in the management of war's booty - our two-legged livestock. Now stop that sniveling and view this as part of your education. To show me you have conquered your childish emotions, I want you to take the whip and finish the boy off until there's not a breath left in him. It will be good for the slaves assembled to see the master's son is a Roman man at his core."

Deeply shamed by his father's disappointment in his character, Centurius had taken the vicious whip and, using all the strength in his young arms, sliced the slave's back to ribbons until, as his father had ordered, the slave boy was obviously dead. When he was finished, Centurius' father wrapped his arms around his exhausted son and announced to the assembled slaves in a prideful voice: "Your young master is fast assuming his place in the world."

The slaves, terrified by the execution of one of their fellow slaves that they had just witnessed, knew enough to cheer for their young master before Centurius turned on one of them with his 'justice.'

"See, Centurius," his father counseled. "Even the slaves are proud of your maturity and will overlook your earlier childish emotionality." He then chuckled. "Imagine getting sick over the whipping of a mere slave. If Romans allowed such childish reactions in themselves, we'd be sick all the time." He guffawed at such an absurdity.

Centurius was a relatively small slaveholder by comparison with other Romans of the day. He only had a little over 300 slaves at this particular farm. Some truly wealthy Romans had herds of slaves numbered in the tens of thousands (drawn from all over the known world) for their various enterprises. The Emperor Vespasian was said to be using over 20,000 slaves captured in his Judean campaigns solely for building the mighty new amphitheater in Rome (later named the Coliseum). Being a small slaveholder allowed him to take a role in the buying, training, discipline and selling of his stock whereas larger slaveholders had agents to do most of this for them. In this respect he was no different than his father before him.

When Centurius bought a slave, he took his time and was careful to check out a property thoroughly before any money changed hands. This meant carefully checking out their bodies from head to toe. He started by running his hands through their hair to check for thickness and texture. Then he checked out their eyes, looking for any diseases that might be harbored there - he knew yellowed eyes spelled trouble over time; then he ran his fingers over their teeth - any who balked at opening wide for his inspection were instantly rejected along with those who had more than two or three rotten or broken teeth. Then he checked out their neck muscles, their shoulder and pectoral muscles, their abdominal muscles and finally their biceps to check for size and strength. Any not well muscled were rejected as unsuitable for the heavy work they would be put to once purchased for his uses. Their feet were carefully checked out one by one, first to check for fallen arches; second to check for knobby toes which told him, an astute buyer, that bone disease might have already started in that piece of stock. Then he checked their ankles carefully for strength and stability; both their calves and their thigh to make sure they were as sturdy as their shoulders and biceps; and, turning the slave around, he kneaded the butt to make sure it was solid muscle and checked out the spine to make sure it was straight and strong. Finally, usually to a slave's total humiliation, he checked out their reproductive organs in case he wanted to breed them. Since all of this took place right on the plinth on which the slave was presented for sale and was usually in a public place, the slave being sold usually blushed in their shame and embarrassment but knew they had to endure the inspection, no matter how they felt about it.

Centurius was careful to make sure his inspections were thorough and gave no thought to how the slave he was inspecting felt about it. He did notice their reactions to the intimate examinations they endured by each and every possible purchaser - any negative reactions to being handled usually meant a firm rejection by the buyer followed by a painful 'on the spot' beating by the dealer. Over the years Centurius figured he had turned down about three-quarters of those he inspected and actually purchased only the remaining one-fourth - those who took to the buyer's handling with ease; who looked like they wanted to be purchased for whatever reason; and those he thought he would have little trouble with once they were his property. In fact, one dealer had labeled him 'a connoisseur of human flesh' - a title he accepted with considerable pride, although he was well aware the dealer was just flattering him to make a sale. Centurius, like almost all Roman masters of his time, never once thought about the plight of that human flesh he was inspecting: the endless inspections by numerous persons (some who had no intentions of actually buying); the humiliation of being examined no different than other livestock up for sale like horses and cows; the shame of usually being examined totally nude no different than other livestock; and the ignominy of never being asked if a total stranger could fondle and manipulate them any way they wanted.

The Thracian slave being disciplined today had endured Centurius' highly personal inspection of his body when they had first met at the slave auction. But he didn't realize then that Centurius also enjoyed being a master in direct charge of his properties and keeping his finger in slave management.

Centurius reasoned that today's 'lesson' to the Thracian slave was what accounted for the few problems he had with his herd of slaves. He also thought that the more all of his slaves knew their master was right there watching over them at all times, making sure they were fed the usual slave gruel, protected from the elements, properly disciplined, and, if necessary, sold off to a possibly far worst plight if they were unappreciative or resentful of his stewardship, the less likely he was to have trouble with any of them. Like most Roman masters, Centurius was well aware fear was absolutely necessary in managing human livestock. Without fear being omnipresent in a slave's life, a master would eventually run into trouble, slaves being what they were.

Centurius thought he represented the best of Roman virtues - stern, disciplined, unwavering, and civilized. His father would be proud of him. Like his father had long ago taught him, fate decided who were masters and who were slaves in the world, and slaves not accepting their god-given fate sometimes needed encouragement to understand their new status. Like most Roman masters he viewed slaves with few exceptions, as 'speaking animals' who were put on this earth to make a better life for whoever purchased them. The more he observed slaves and their animalistic behavior, their ready response to the whip, their clamoring for even scraps of food, their eagerness to mate at the slightest opportunity and their solicitous groveling for favors he was convinced slaves looked like humans, may have once been free, but with enslavement they became a servile race of their own. Of course, slaves to the manor (born to slave mothers) knew their status from birth; those newly enslaved had to be 'broken' to their new status, similar to a wild horse.

Over the years Canis, who had once been of free status in Transalpine Gaul, had trouble even remembering when he had been free and made all of his own decisions. But fate had placed him with Centurius, his current master, and he was determined to make the best of it. Despite the collar around his neck and the tell-tale ownership brand on his rump and shoulder telling the world he was the property of Centurius, he still had obtained some status despite his humiliating slave name as his master's steward, certainly a high position compared to the stable hands, and which gave him a degree of coveted authority over those even lower down the chain than he was. Nevertheless, he had to be careful at all times to do exactly as his master wished, do it as quickly as possible, and never question his master on any matter, even when he knew his master was wrong.

Canis was far wiser than his master ever suspected. He knew being an owner of hundreds of slaves had its temptations along with increased responsibilities. Many slave masters, surrounded by fawning sycophants (such as himself) willing to fulfill their every wish began to believe they were as omnipotent and god-like as the slaves who they had the power of life and death over had led them to believe. Indeed some masters had tortuously killed their slaves for even the most minor offenses simply because they could do so, despite the obvious costs of such arrogance. Some slave masters allowed themselves to sink into slothful laziness, letting their slaves do even the most insignificant personal tasks for them, e.g., some slave masters no longer bathed themselves, let alone dressed themselves. Such practices led to a dependence on slave labor which often left the master helpless on his own. Canis also realized that having absolute power over others was addictive (as a steward over other slaves he realized this applied to him as well as his master) and dulls one's ability to negotiate normal social relations, let alone the ability to supervise and lead the free - it's always harder to convince than order. And Canis was as guilty as Centurius in satisfying his own sexual desires through those under his authority. He wondered if masters ever thought of how difficult it was to maintain a satisfying marriage when a sexual whim could be satisfied by a master of mistress with the mere snap of a finger. Canis in his younger years had caught the eye of his mistress and had little choice outside of pleasing her, although as a slave it was illegal for him to ever marry. But these observations had to be kept to himself - to share them with his master would not only be outrageously presumptuous but an effrontery to any master, not just his own.

Several weeks later Centurius decided to 'cull' his herd which led to numerous examinations of slave's bodies in determining who would be sold off and who would be retained. Selected for sale were aging slaves, slaves who had proved troublesome, slaves who had acquired some disability over the years, slaves unseemly in appearance, slaves who had proven infertile in the farm's breeding operations, and very attractive young slaves who had been bred for market right there on his property and were too valuable for mere labor purposes. They would be replaced with fresh purchases at the local slave market that were young, healthy, and had the promise of a lifetime of hard labor in their bodies. Centurius could feel the apprehension of the slaves being examined - they were well aware of why their bodies were being probed and prodded.

"Please, master, don't sell me off, master," a few dared to plead, fearing the mines or the galleys lay ahead of them, a sure guarantee of a relatively short life.

Centurius offered the anxious slaves some wise counsel. "A slave's life is like the wind - always changing - so you don't know what direction you will be taken. A slave can live his whole life with a single master or have a dozen masters before he dies. He could be a mistress' pampered houseboy or victim of the cruelest taskmaster's brutal whip. He may die tomorrow at the whim of a callous master or live out a full life under a kindly master little different than a stern and demanding father. Fate decides a slave's life just as fate has decided he is a slave. Whatever lies ahead for you, slave, accept it as fate's destiny for you and accept it without objection. There are no other options for a slave."

Those slaves being examined realized every word their master said was absolutely true and became silent as their bodies continued to be inspected in the most intimate ways. The whole world as they knew it had slaves no different than themselves, being bought and sold just like cattle, and fulfilling their master's demands without question.

CELIA, AN AMERICAN SLAVE

Mid 19th Century

Celia felt the pangs of labor increase as she trudged back from the cotton fields to her cabin. If she could just hold that new baby in until Mudge, the burly slave midwife could be found to help deliver her seventh offspring.

Celia, a large-boned sturdy woman, was in her 21st year by her reckoning and had first been placed with Big Sam when she first showed some signs of her emerging womanhood around 13. She still remembered how scared she had been then, never having been with a man before, and with Mr. Perkins, Master Jenkins' nasty old overseer, watching the two of them 'go at it' as he had ordered with a leering smirch on his face. Since that time long ago, she had been put under Big Sam every time she wasn't knocked up, along with most of the other wenches on the plantation. Big Sam's seed must be responsible for a good 50 of the young-in's running around the cabins by now.

As soon as Celia reached the door of her cabin, she was relieved to see Mudge hastening across the yard. Celia had never had her help before, but the other slave women all spoke admiringly of her skills in helping them deliver their 'git.'

"Pleased to meet you," Celia said as she gasped and headed for the rickety old cot in her cabin.

"Pleased to be met," Mudge responded as she quickly got Celia's clothes off of her and her legs spread wide. "It'll all be over in just a few minutes, the way you'se breathin."

Mudge was right. Within an hour it was all over and yet another 'property' had been added to the plantation's register - this time a shiny black boy looking as healthy as could be. Celia marveled at how perfect he was and whether she'd get to look after him for long or if Master Jenkins would sell him off as soon as he could walk. Of the six she'd birthed for Master Jenkins so far, only three of them were still around - two had died early and one had been sold off already to a passing slave trader who was looking for stock he could buy cheap, raise on in his own 'slave farm' over in Alabama and then sell them off for a good price. Even Celia knew slaves were going up in price. She had heard Master Jenkins bragging to some visitors he was making as much money raising slaves now as he was raising cotton, especially since the land was slowly playing out with over 50 years of cotton plantings since his pappy first started the plantation with just a handful of slaves.

"More money in niggers than in cotton," he had practically whispered to those he trusted since discussion on that topic was considered uncouth and not proper for polite society.

Outside of being pregnant most of the time since she was 14, Celia's daylight hours were spent mainly out in the cotton fields, dragging the big bag behind her where slaves put the white fluffy bolls they plucked off the cotton plants one by one. Men and women slaves worked side by side and each had to make their quota for the day - 60# in the bag at the end of the work day for a man; 50# for the women slaves - unless they wanted their rations of corn meal, beans, rice and bacon rinds cut. Master Jenkins was proud of operating on the 'quota system' where each slave had a measurable work goal for the day. That scale at the side of the field determined whether your belly would get anything in it or not at the end of the long 12-hour day. Still, Master Jenkins wasn't one to tolerate laziness in his niggers, anyone not busy picking except for the noon break could expect the overseers whip on his back soon enough. That ol' peckerwood overseer prancing around on his horse out in the fields seems to like nothing better than to whip a slave anytime he had an excuse.

Celia especially hated the smelly white boss man with his big paunch hanging over his belt because several times he had ordered her over to the bushes aside the fields and taken his pleasure with her. One of those times he had knocked her up and she had yielded a baby as bright as an octoroon. Such offspring always had special problems - the black slaves didn't take to them too well because they were different and reminded them of the whites who owned them and the white women didn't like them one bit because it reminded them that a lot of white men were taking advantage of their female slaves, most of those white men were probably married. Even Celia knew the states had laws against whites and blacks fooling around with each other, but that was one law that seemed to be overlooked unless a black male even looked at a white female in which case the poor slave was usually hung or shot on the spot as an example to others.

Most of her life Celia had done nothing but plant cotton, weed cotton, pick cotton and tend the vegetable garden she shared with the other slave women. Sometimes she had a man in her cabin but sometimes not - Big Sam and her got along real well and although slaves weren't allowed to marry, the men tended to pick a favorite woman who then cooked for them, mended their clothes, and gave them company. In return, Big Sam warmed her bed when the overseer didn't order him to the barn for his 'other duties', chopped her wood, kept her cabin in repair, and helped out with the kids.

Like most of the other adult male slaves, Big Sam did the heavy work: loading the cotton bales (100# each), lugging the cotton bags from the fields to the gin, clearing the forests, and draining the swamps. Celia marveled how he had any strength left in him at all by the time the sun set despite his big build and huge musculature. A slave like him cost twice as much as her at almost any market, despite the fact she had proven to be a good breeder. Over their years together, Celia found out Big Sam hated his 'other duties', especially when he knew the results would all be sold off as soon as they were of market age. He didn't even know who half of them were anymore since some of their mothers had since been sold off, some of the mothers didn't want their offspring to know their daddy had been 'arranged' by the overseer, and some mothers turned their resentment toward him rather than the master who had treated them no different than his other livestock when it came to multiplying the herd.

Celia (nor Big Sam) knew little of life outside the plantation they were on. When there were rumors among the slaves about some blacks running off to be free up North on something they called the 'underground railroad' it meant nothing to her. She couldn't imagine sneaking off to the 'north' - other than following the stars she would have no idea of how to get there, how far it was, or what she would find once she was there. She couldn't even imagine being 'free' although the idea was intriguing. Imagine living with any man you wanted; getting married like white folk; being paid for your work; having babies when you and your chosen man decided; not having an overseer whipping your back open just because you stopped work for a drink of water; and visiting a place over the hill just because you were curious as to what was there. It sounded like the 'heaven' white folk were always talking about, but Celia couldn't help but worry about where she would live outside of her master's shack, how she would feed her babies if the master didn't provide the food, and who would want a woman who only knew how to tend the cotton fields and have babies. The more she thought about it, the whole idea of running didn't seem as if it was ever going to happen, especially when the few who tried it were either shot on the spot, gnarled by the master's dogs, or whipped until they might as well have been dead with the master's vicious bullwhip reserved for just such offenses. Besides, it would be hard to leave her babies even though she knew they weren't really hers and would be sold off no later than when they were full grown.

One day Master Jenkins brought a white man down to where all the slave shacks were and told them this white man was going to give them 'religion' just like the white folks had. Reverend Smith, as this man called himself, explained to them about Jesus and going to heaven. He said Jesus loved each and every one of them, even though he was white, and if they made a hard effort to be 'good niggers' and did exactly what they were told without any lip or resentment, that they would go to a special slave heaven where there wouldn't be master or overseers like on this earth, but where they could do what they wanted. But only if they did exactly what was expected of black folk while in this world - working hard and obeying without question. If you didn't do that, then you went to Hell when you died where you would be beaten all the time with a bullwhip, have your tongue ripped out of your head, worked like you'd never been worked before and finally be burnt alive. Reverend Smith came every Sunday night after that and Master Jenkins ordered all of them to listen to 'every word' that came out of his mouth - it was the Holy Word the Reverend was speaking and Master Jenkins was being especially solicitous to hire him for the slaves' benefit. Celia listened as ordered and liked the idea of a white man caring about her, but didn't think much of the rest of it. If this Jesus was such a great man why did he let his black children be treated like animals while white folk lived off their sweat? Reverend Smith even had an answer for that: black people were condemned in the Holy Bible to serve others as slaves and should just accept God's will in this matter. But Celia liked the 'hymns' Reverend Smith introduced them to and found some of them quite tuneful. She had always liked to sing and quickly turned the new tunes into something of her own liking which the white folk called 'spirituals' not understanding the black slaves were mainly singing about being free of the whites someday.

Celia and Big Sam lived together for a good 20 more years after they had first met. Celia by then had produced over 19 babies for her master but only 5 of them were still around. A few had been sold off to itinerant slave dealers passing through, most had gone off in wagons to the big markets in the large cities as the 'annual crop' as soon as they started turning into men; a few had died of malnutrition or yellow fever, dysentery, and diphtheria; and the five remaining had already been assigned chores right here on Master Jenkins' plantation. Big Sam had sired more children than he could keep track of, but the only ones he cared about were those he had with Celia. It broke his heart as much as it did Celia's when yet another one of their progeny was sold, never to be seen again.

Eventually both Celia and Big Sam were simply worn out. Big Sam died one day in the fields. He slumped over while hoisting cotton bags up into the wagons and even the current overseer's constant whip couldn't get him up on his feet. He died within minutes right out in the blazing sun in the very field he had first worked in as a small child. The current Master Jenkins (the old master's son) buried him in the area where old slaves were disposed of and no money was wasted on a gravestone that would identify the exact spot.

Celia grieved for seven years after that as did the children of their union until those children too were eventually sold off to new owners far away. Every chance she had she put some wild flowers on where she thought Big Sam's body probably was. She was barren now, so Master Jenkins didn't assign her another partner but she took in one of the older men slaves who had proven as barren as she was now. She liked cooking and mending for him, but it wasn't the same as when Big Sam was around. That cold rainy winter, Celia along with four other old slaves, got the 'croup'. When the five of them didn't have the strength to go out to the field, Master Jenkins himself came to their cabins with the local veterinarian, not with a whip as would be normal when you didn't make it to the fields, but with a bottle of medicine.[Slaves didn't have doctors, but veterinarians looked after them like other livestock].

"Take this, Celia," the veterinarian said kindly as he poured out a spoonful and pressed it to the prone slave's lips. "This will put you out of your misery."

Celia knew what was in that bottle. She knew of other old sick slaves the master had given it to and they never woke up. It was called 'laudanum' (an opiate derivative) or something like that and was in most every veterinary's medicine bag to handle the chronically ill and the disabled. Celia swallowed it down with relief. She was tired of her life, she missed Big Sam, and thought maybe in this black heaven the white folk talked about she could see some of her children that had been sold off over the years.

Soon after, Celia was buried in the slave pit not far from Big Sam's remains and like him, no grave marker identifies the spot.

References & Suggested Readings

Adams, P., Langer, E., Hwa, L., Stearns, P. & Wiesner-Hanks, M. (2000). *Experiencing world history.* NY: NYU Press [interesting sections on Chinese and other Asian slavery].

Bradley, K. R. (2008). *Slavery and society in Rome.* Cambridge: Cambridge University Press.

Bradley, K. R. (1989). *Slaves and masters in the Roman Empire: A study in social control.* Oxford: Oxford University Press.

Davis, Robert C. (2003). *Christian slaves, Muslim masters: white slavery in the Mediterranean, the Barbary Coast and Italy, 1500-1800.* New York: Palgrave MacMillan.

Degler, C. N. (1986). *Neither black nor white: slavery and relations in Brazil and the United States.* Madison, WI: University of Wisconsin Press.

Engerman, S. L. & Fogel, R. W.(1974) *Time on the cross: the economics of American slavery.* NY: Little Brown and Company.

Fisher, H. J. (2001). *Slavery in the history of Muslim Black Africa.* New York: New York University Press.

Finley, M. I. (2003). *Classical slavery.* London: Routledge.

Fogel, R. W. (1994). *Without consent or contract: the rise and fall of American slavery.* New York: W. W. Norton & Company.

Gordon, M. (1989). *Slavery in the Arab world.* New York: New Amsterdam Books [originally published in France as *l'Esclavage dans le monde arabe*]

Hellie, R. (1984). *Slavery in Russia.* Chicago: University of Chicago Press.

Hopkins, K. (2010). *Conquerors and slaves: sociological studies in Roman history, Vol. I.* Cambridge: Cambridge University Press.

Kim, Hyong-In (2009). *American and Asian slavery: slave life in Antebellum South Carolina and early Choseon Korea (American University Series I4, History).* NY: Peter Land Publishing.

Laffin, J. (1982). *The Arabs as master slavers.* Englewood, NJ: SBS Publishing [Mainly about slavery in the 20th century.]

Milgram, S. (1974). *Obedience to authority.* New York: Harper.

Milgram, S. (1963). *Behavioral study of obedience,* Journal of Abnormal and Social Psychology, 67, 371-378.

Patterson, O. (1985). *Slavery and social death: a comparative study.* Cambridge: Harvard University Press.

Rawson, B. (1989). *The family in ancient Rome: new perspectives.* Ithaca, NY: Cornell University Press.

Segal, R. (2001). *Islam's black slaves.* New York: Farrar, Straus and Giroux.

Soper, R. (2008). *World slavery, the bigger picture.* New York: BookSurge Publishing.

Ste Croix, G. E .M . de (1975). *Early Christian attitudes toward property and slavery.* Studies in Church History, 12, 1-38.

Ste Croix, G. E .M . de (1998). *The class struggle in the Ancient Greek World: from the Archaic Age to the Arab conquests*. Ithaca, NY: Cornell University Press.

Thomas, F. C. (2001). *Slavery and Jihad in the Sudan*. Bloomington, IN: iUniverse, Inc.

Vogt, J. (1978). *Ancient slavery and the idea of man*. New York: Wiley Blackwell [out of print].

Walvin, J. (2007). *The trader, the owner, the slave*. London: Vintage Books [Mainly on the Atlantic trade in black slaves].

Westerman, W. L. (1974). *Slave systems of Greek and Roman antiquity*. New York: American Philosophical Society.

About The Author

Harve E. Rawson was raised in the Ozark Mountains of Southern Missouri and worked for 15 months following his high school graduation prior to entering Antioch College (Ohio) where he obtained his B.A. degree. He then proceeded to Ohio State University where he received his Ph.D. degree four years later, having been named the Ohio State Scholar. He then worked as a research scientist on Project Apollo but ultimately ended up as a college professor of psychology at Hanover College (Indiana) where he remained for 32 years. During that long tenure, he was named a Fulbright Scholar twice and taught for a year in Bahrain. He then moved on to become Dean of Faculty and then Acting Dean of the College at Franklin College and, later, a visiting professor of psychology at Mississippi State University.

Raised in the 'slave' state of Missouri, he experienced race segregation first hand as a child, heard stories regarding the times of slavery, and later visited many areas of the world where slavery in its various forms had been widely practiced. As a psychologist, he developed a strong interest in how slaves were controlled, how slaves dealt with their lack of freedom, the psychological price of their slavery, and why most slaves' attempts to free themselves failed. Following this interest, he avariciously read everything he could on historical slavery and soon realized how little information was available from the viewpoint of the slaves themselves (most slaves couldn't read or write and no one in power was interested in their perspective anyway). It was not surprising historians authored most of the books on slavery and carefully followed what few sources they had available to them, many of which were written by slave holders themselves who tended to justify ownership of other humans accordingly.

Dr. Rawson emphasizes that this book was designed as a supplemental reading for a world history course (or anyone interested in the topic of global slavery) and aspires to give a more psychological view of slavery, attempts to view slavery from a slave's perspective, and examines various myths and other disciplines' viewpoints of holding humans in bondage. He asserts he certainly makes no attempt to cover all aspects of slavery nor offer the typical scholarly thoroughness on the subject. It is simply a primer on world slavery to give the reader a quick overview of man's worst crime against humanity - slavery.

Dr. Rawson is a recent widower after 47 years of marriage, has two sons, and currently lives near Atlanta, Georgia.

OTHER BOOKS BY THE AUTHOR

If you enjoyed this book, you might also enjoy other books by this author delivered right from the publisher to your door for the lowest price and quickest delivery.

"*Webb City*," life in an Ozark mining town in the Great Depression and World War II as seen through the eyes of a small boy. (Xlibris. 2000) [Order by calling 1-888-795-4274]

"*Around the World in 30 Years*," a compendium of travel tales covering everything from living in Bahrain to crossing the Andes by train to visiting China in the time of Chairman Mao. (Xlibris, 2000) [Order by calling 1-888-795-4274]

"*The Itinerant Slave*," a time-travel fiction describing the life of a slave in Ancient Rome, the Antebellum American South, and the early 20th century Middle East, written under the pseudonym Jacque Aaronsen . (Xlibris, 2000) [Order by calling 1-888-795-4274]

"*Purposeful Parenting: A Practical Guide for Today's World*,"critically acclaimed; covering 32 critical issues affecting all parents at one time or another in the rearing of their children. (AuthorHouse, 2002) [Order by calling 1-888-280-7715]

"*A Delightful Ordeal: Travel Tales That Teach*," a fascinating and insightful analysis of 18 unusual destinations throughout the world that is the next best thing to being there yourself. This book proves conclusively that travel is the world's best teacher.(AuthorHouse, 2003). [Order by calling 1-888-280-7715]

"Travels of an Iconoclast: An American Psychologist's Perspective on Countries That Best Illustrate World Problems." Thirty nations illustrate contemporary world problems that have been successfully addressed or accommodated. (AuthorHouse, 2005) [Order by calling 1-888-280-7715]

"Buried in the Ivy: A Professor's Odyssey Through a Private Liberal Arts College." What students taught a professor over a 35 year period. (AuthorHouse, 2007) [Order by calling 1-888-280-7715]

"Dying in Egypt: A Remarkable Tale of Death and its Complexities." Losing your beloved spouse in an alien land is devastating but dealing with grief successfully is even more challenging. (AuthorHouse, 2009) [Order by calling 1-888-280-7715]

All major credit cards are accepted from the publishers above.

www.ingramcontent.com/pod-product-compliance
Lightning Source LLC
Chambersburg PA
CBHW030401290526
45785CB00004B/1854